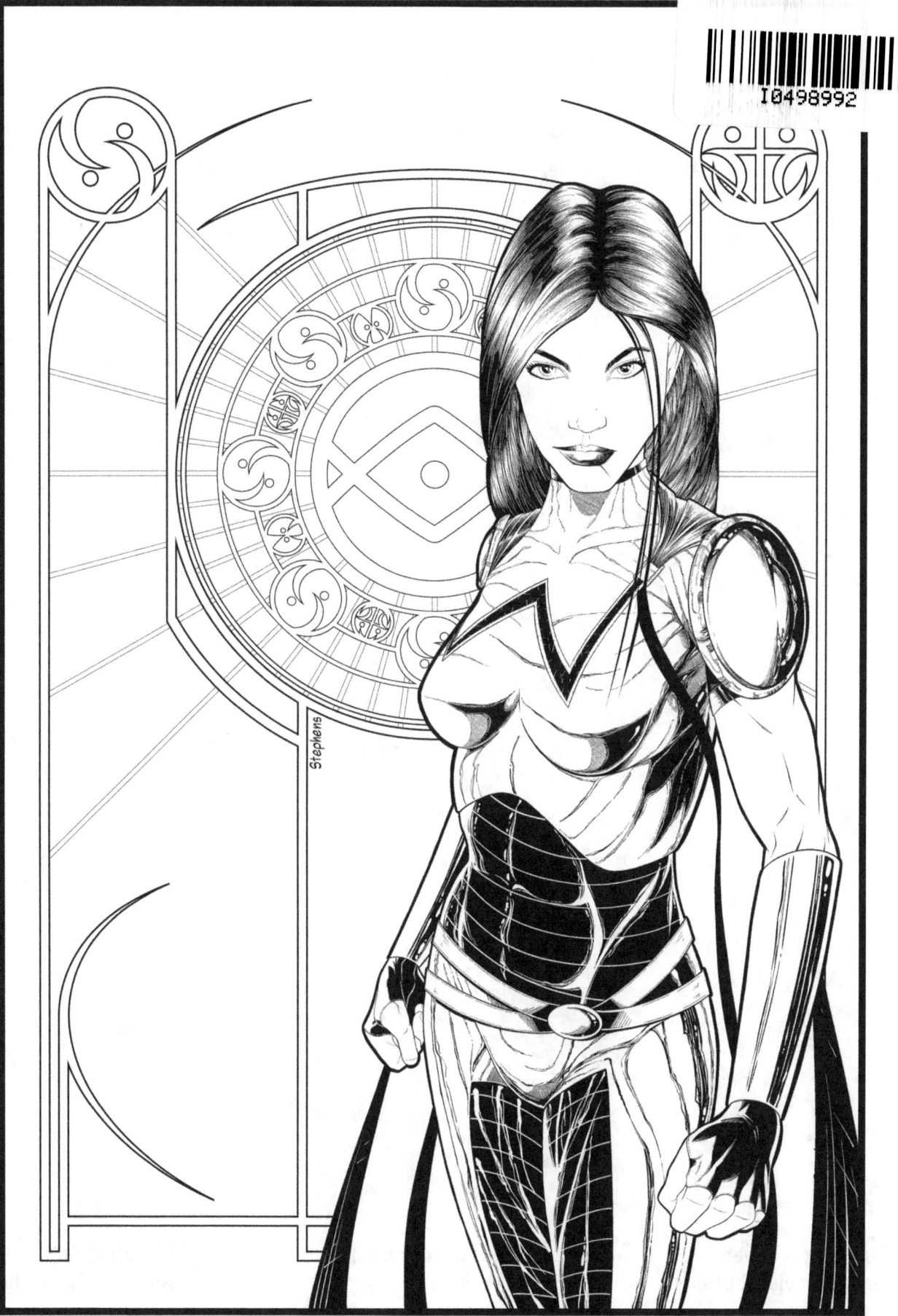

Shinjū Prelude Cover
Lineart by Travis Stephens

Tag us in your posts!
@kaishostudios

© 2020 Kaisho Studios
www.kaishostudios.com

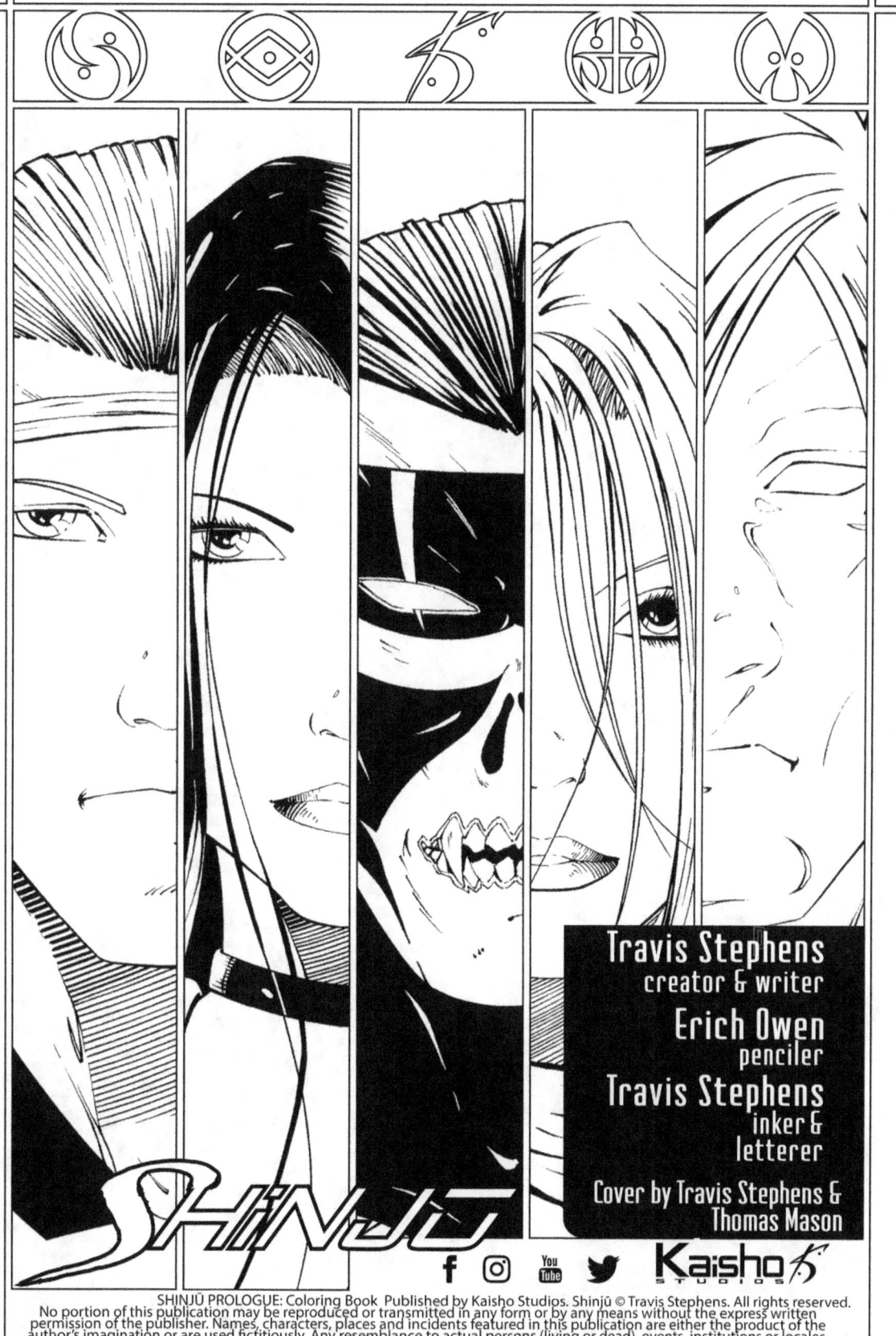

Shinjū Prelude Credits
Lineart by Travis Stephens

Tag us in your posts!
@kaishostudios

© 2020 Travis Stephens
www.kaishostudios.com

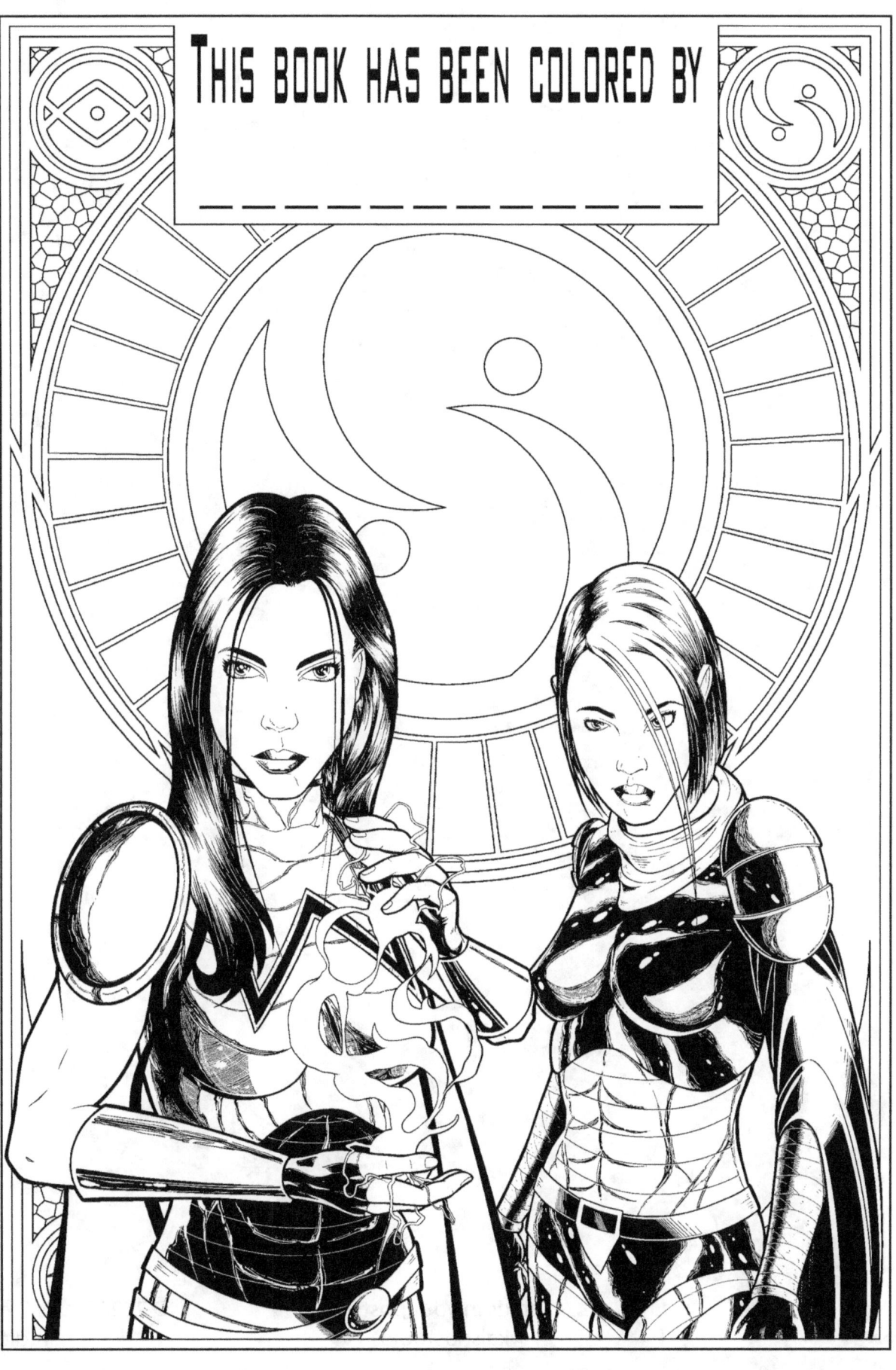

Shinjū Prelude

Tag us in your posts!
@kaishostudios

© 2020 Travis Stephens
www.kaishostudios.com

COLOR TEST PAGE

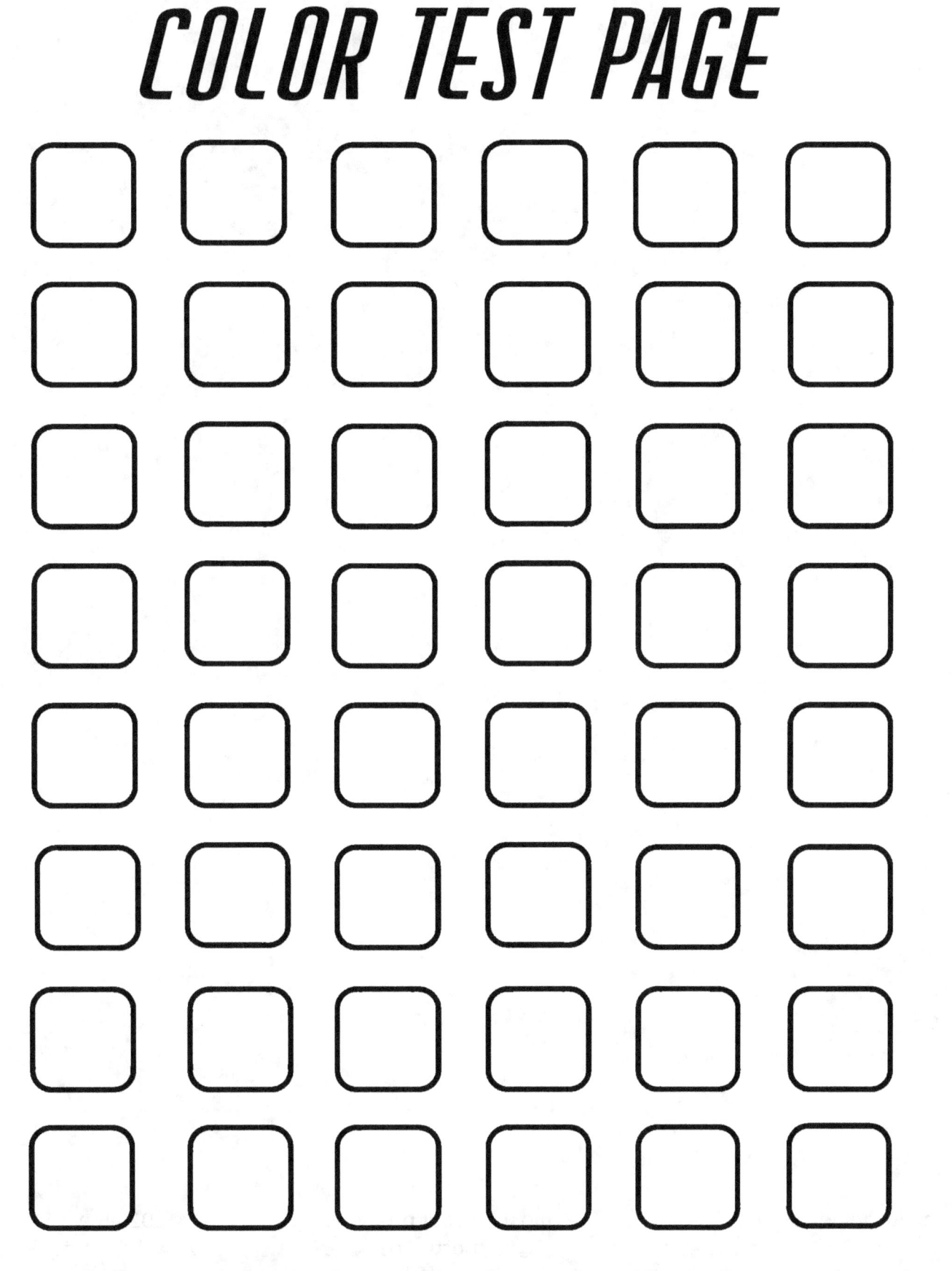

Shinjū Prelude

Tag us in your posts!
@kaishostudios

© 2020 Travis Stephens
www.kaishostudios.com

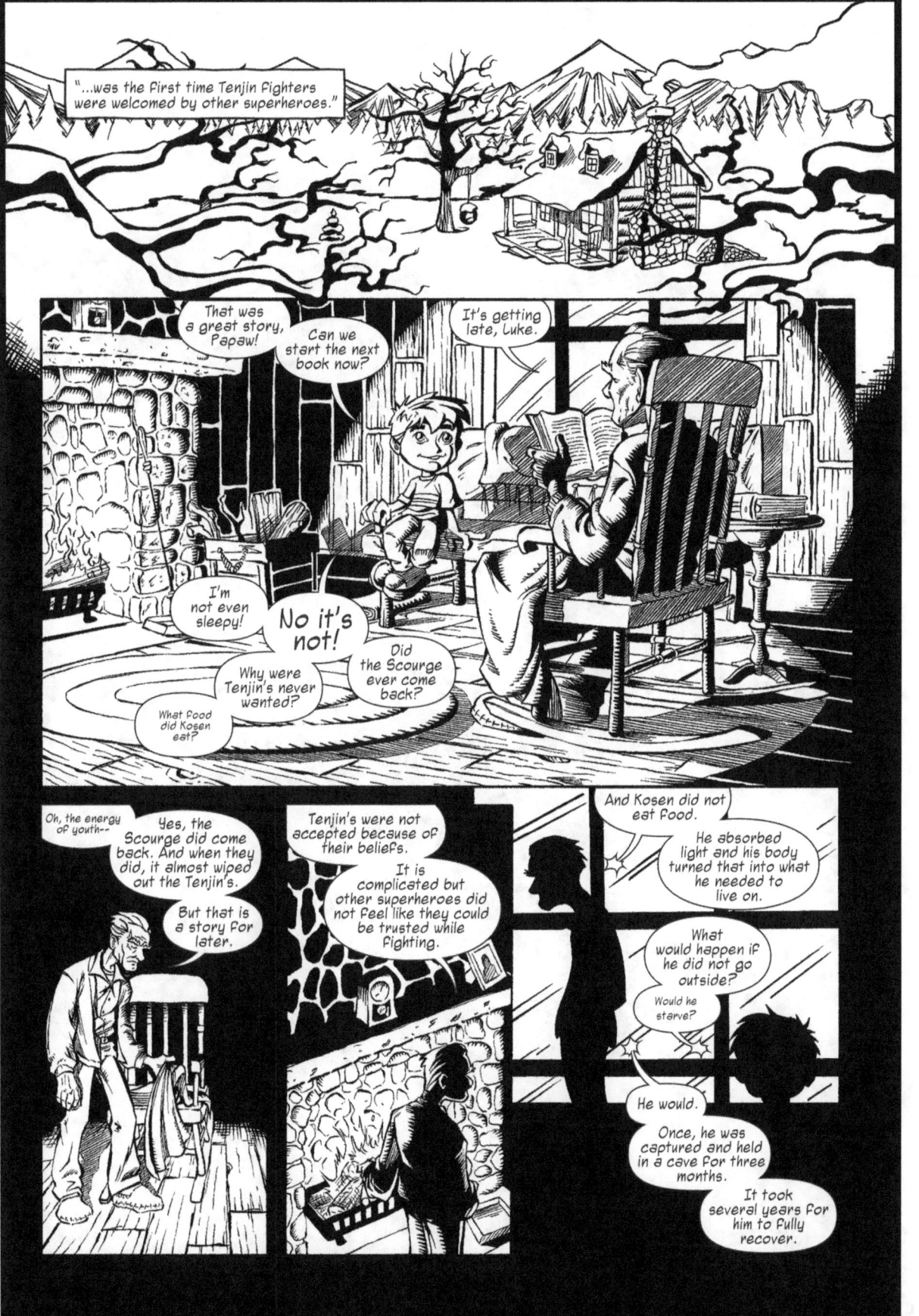

Shinjū Prelude Page 01
Lineart by Erich Owen and
Travis Stephens

Tag us in your posts!
@kaishostudios

© 2020 Travis Stephens
www.kaishostudios.com

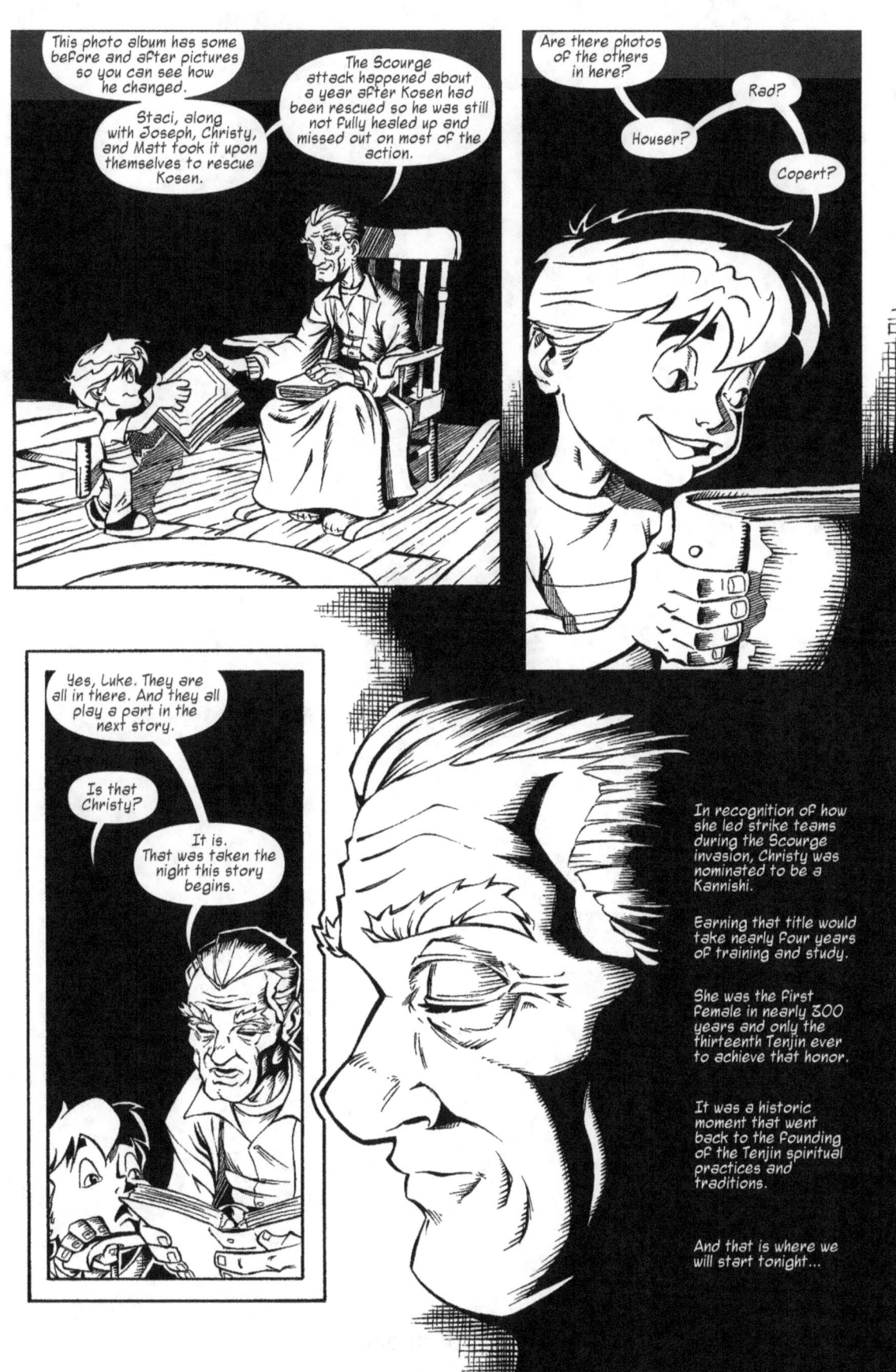

Shinjū Prelude Page 02
Lineart by Erich Owen and
Travis Stephens

© 2020 Travis Stephens
www.kaishostudios.com

CWEZI

Cwezi-Ancient Gods that reside in the mountains of Uganda.

The Cwezi are responsible for judging the readiness of Tenjin followers by overseeing the Unifailia ceremony.

Mukami presides over the Cleansing Ceremony, ensuring corrupted souls are housed in worthy Banyoro hosts.

Ten'ja-A disciple of the Cwezi that helped spread their message throughout the world.

Ujin'ce-A disciple of the Cwezi that helped spread their message throughout the world.

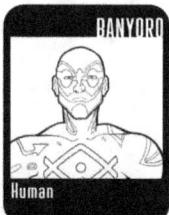
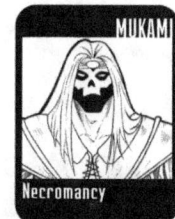
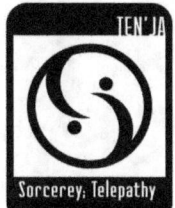
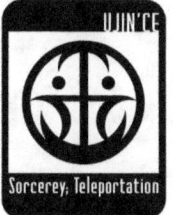

TENJIN

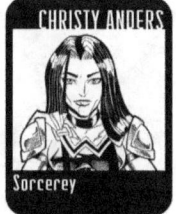
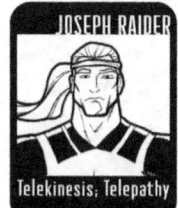

Tenjin-Followers of the Cwezi disciple Ten'ja.

She became a God herself when she defeated Ujin'ce during the Jūjigun, which led to the splintering of the Cwezi followers, creating the Tenjin sect.

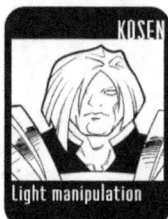
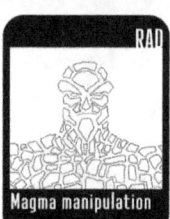
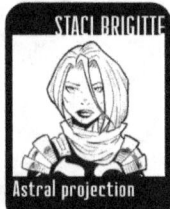
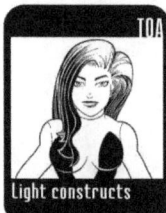

UJIKIRA

Ujikira-Followers of the Cwezi disciple Ujin'ce.

He was cast out from the Cwezi, which led to the Jūjigun, splintering the Cwezi followers and the creation of the Ujikira sect.

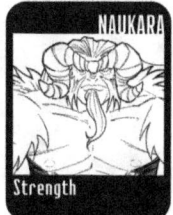
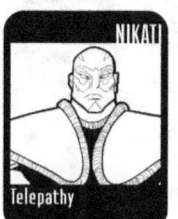

Shinjū Prelude Page 02
Lineart by Erich Owen and Travis Stephens

© 2020 Travis Stephens
www.kaishostudios.com

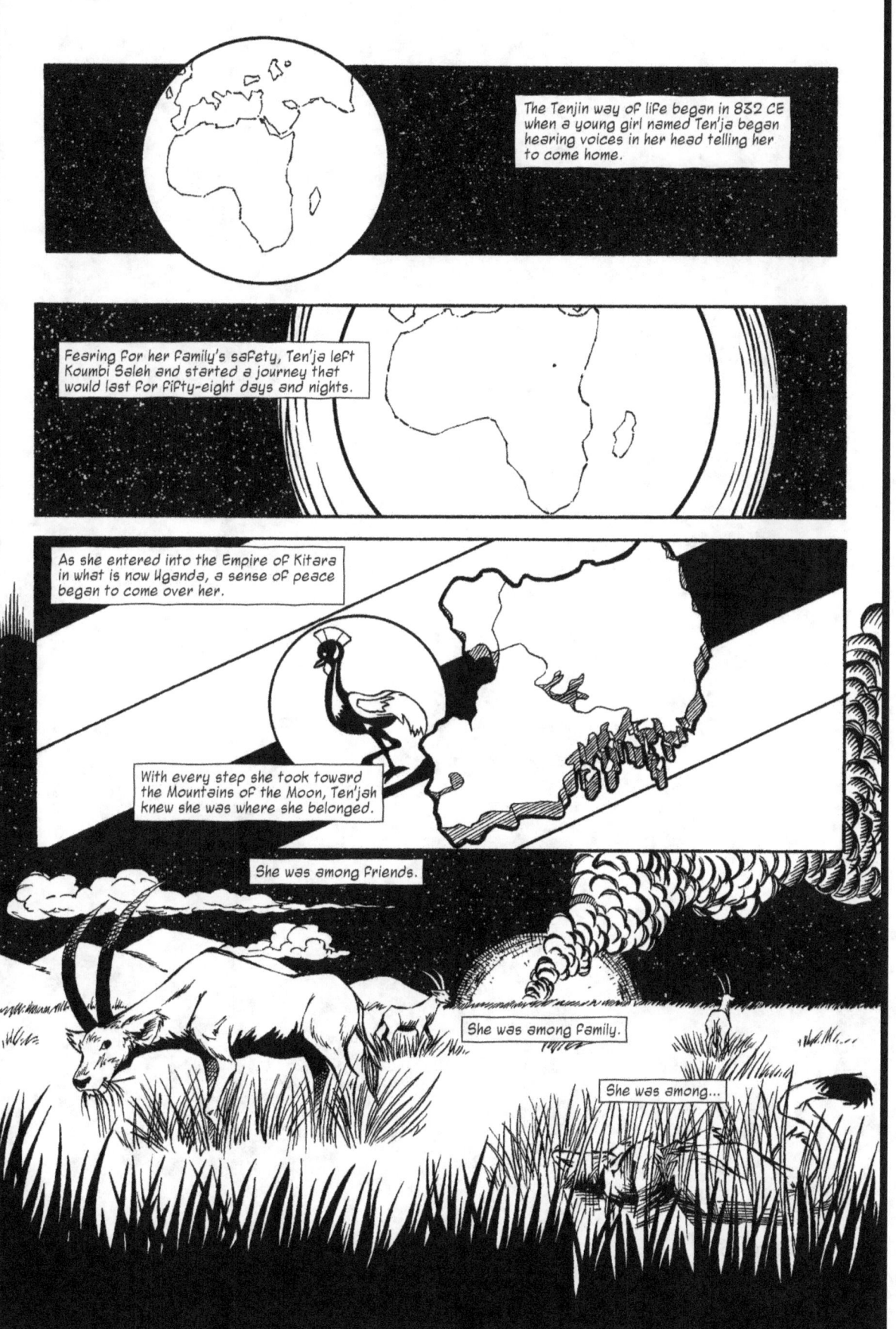

Shinjū Prelude Page 03
Lineart by Erich Owen and Travis Stephens

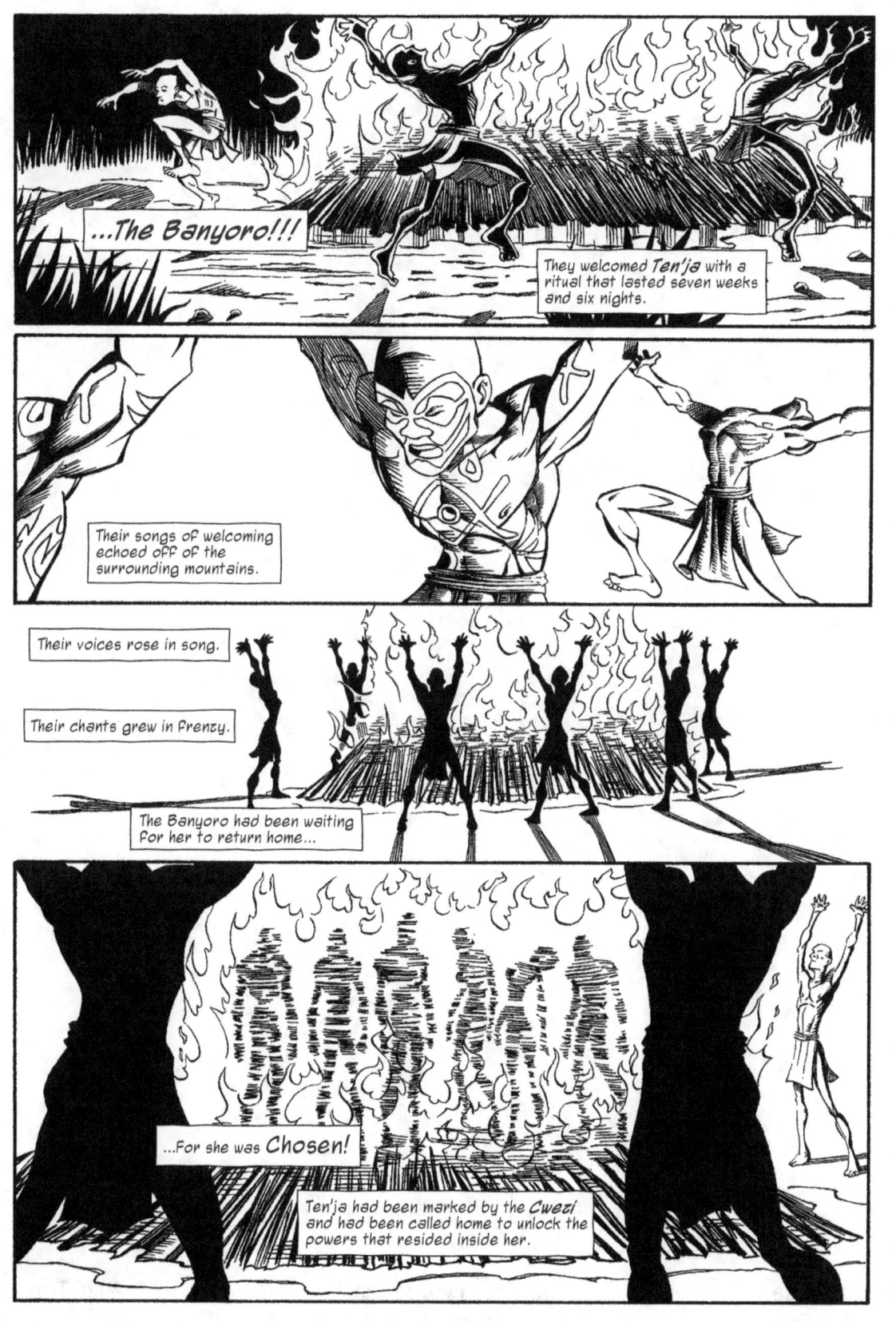

Shinjū Prelude Page 04
Lineart by Erich Owen and Travis Stephens

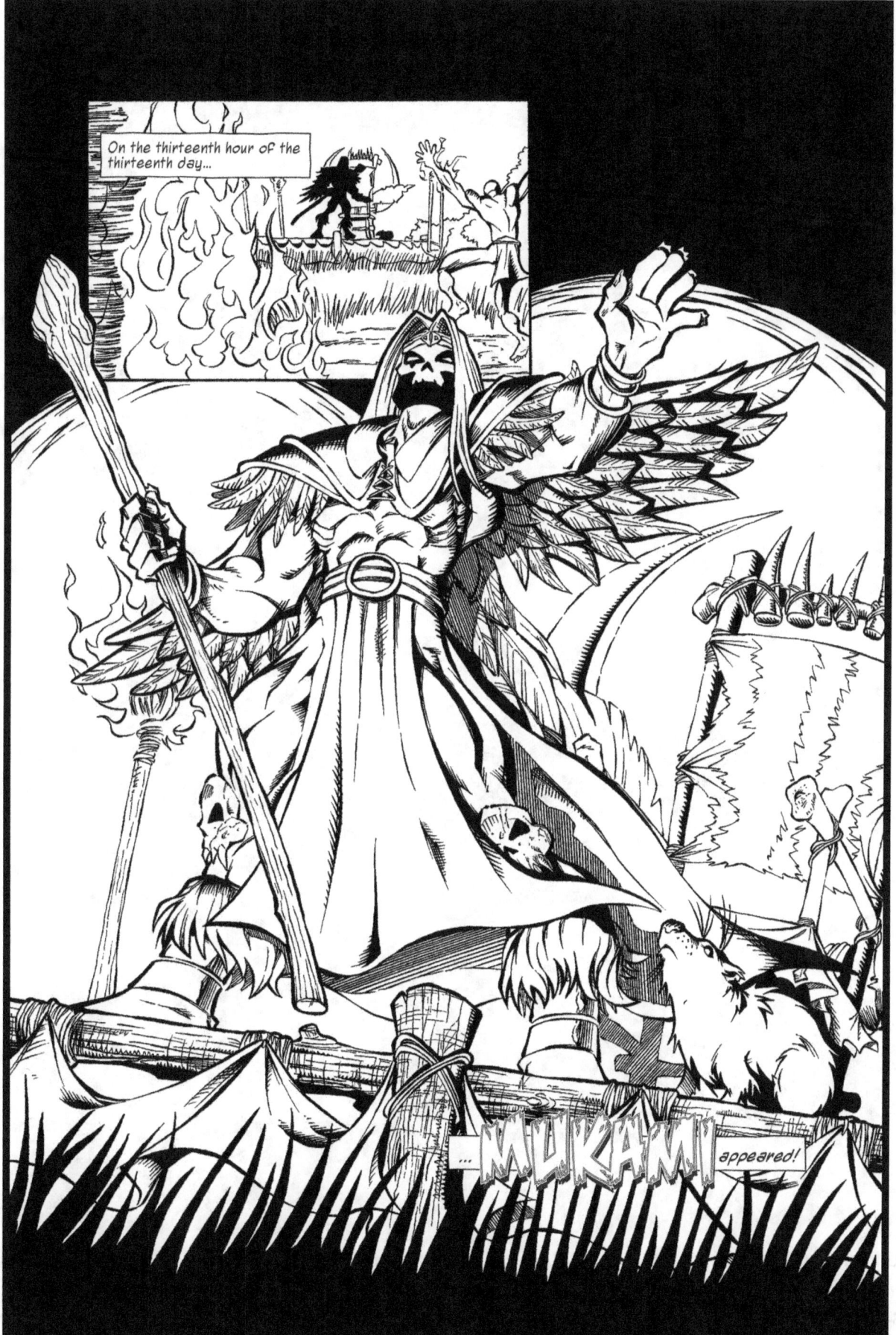

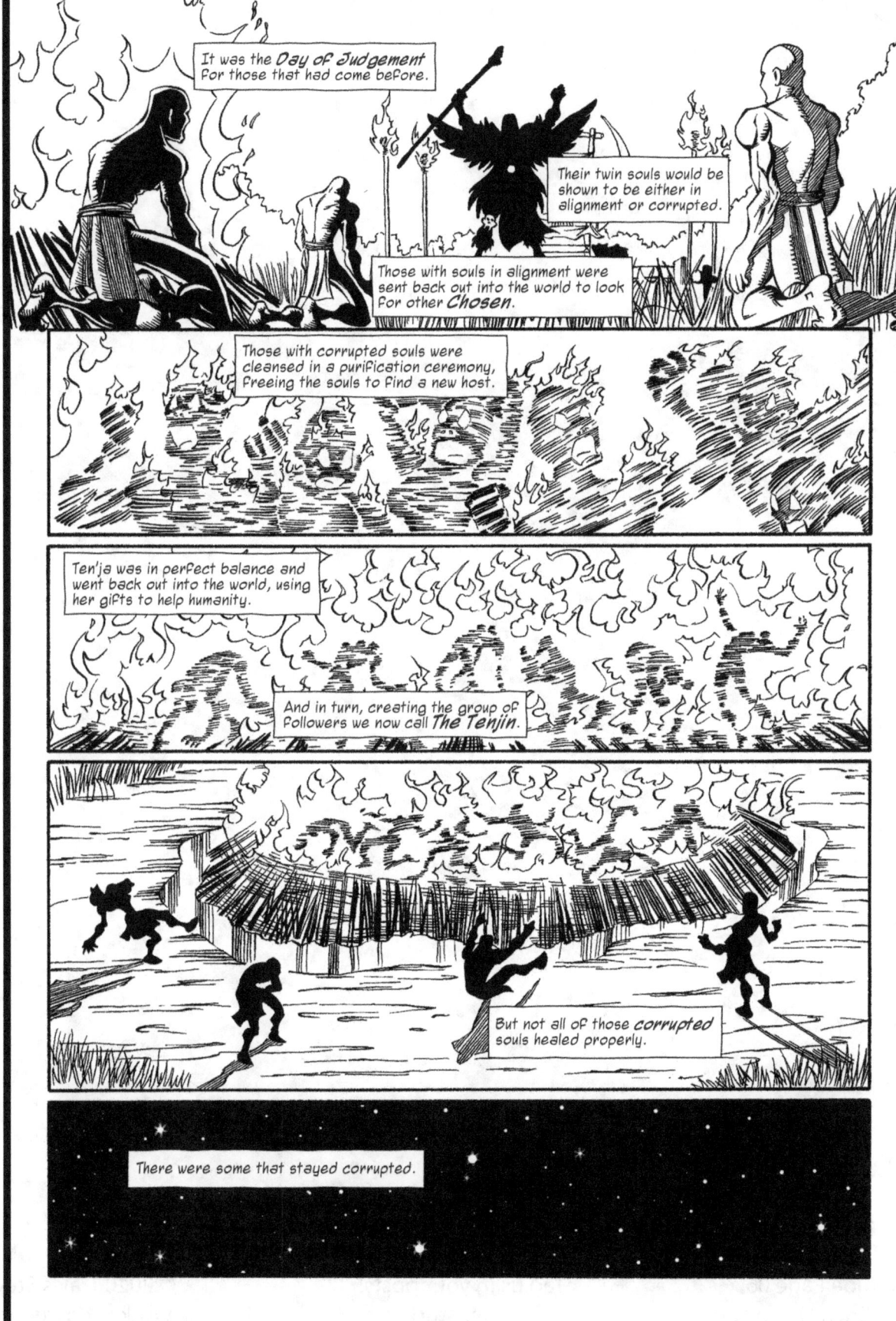

Pacific Estate,
Crawford, Colorado

"When I was a kid, my mom would take me and my sister on weekend trips to Rottnest Island so we could see the stars.

"Mom would point out the constellations and I would dream about one day being up there.

"Now, I *have* been up there.

"I've *been* to the moon, to *other planets*, fought many fights for people that will *never know* I exist.

"I've been to the outer reaches of space.

"But this view, the view of these stars from right here on Earth, is the most *beautiful* sight I have ever seen."

Joseph, I'm scared I'll never see it again. What if I'm not ready for the *Unifailia?* What happens if I don't make it through?

What if it *changes* me physically? Like *Rad, Kosen,* or--

IF it does--

--you will still be *you*. You will still be *Christy Anders*, badass Tenjin sorceress.

All the Unifailia does is test your souls to see if they are living in harmony.

The way you carry yourself shows that they *are*.

Do you really think *Augury* would send you if she didn't think you were ready?

I don't know. *Maybe?*

But it's not just that.

Augury says I am to be a *Kanneshi*. There have only been *twelve* of those!

Hundreds of Tenjin have taken the *Trials* and only *twelve* have been deemed worthy of that title!

Am *I* worthy of that?

Shinjū Prelude Page 07
Lineart by Erich Owen and
Travis Stephens

Tag us in your posts!
@kaishostudios

© 2020 Travis Stephens
www.kaishostudios.com

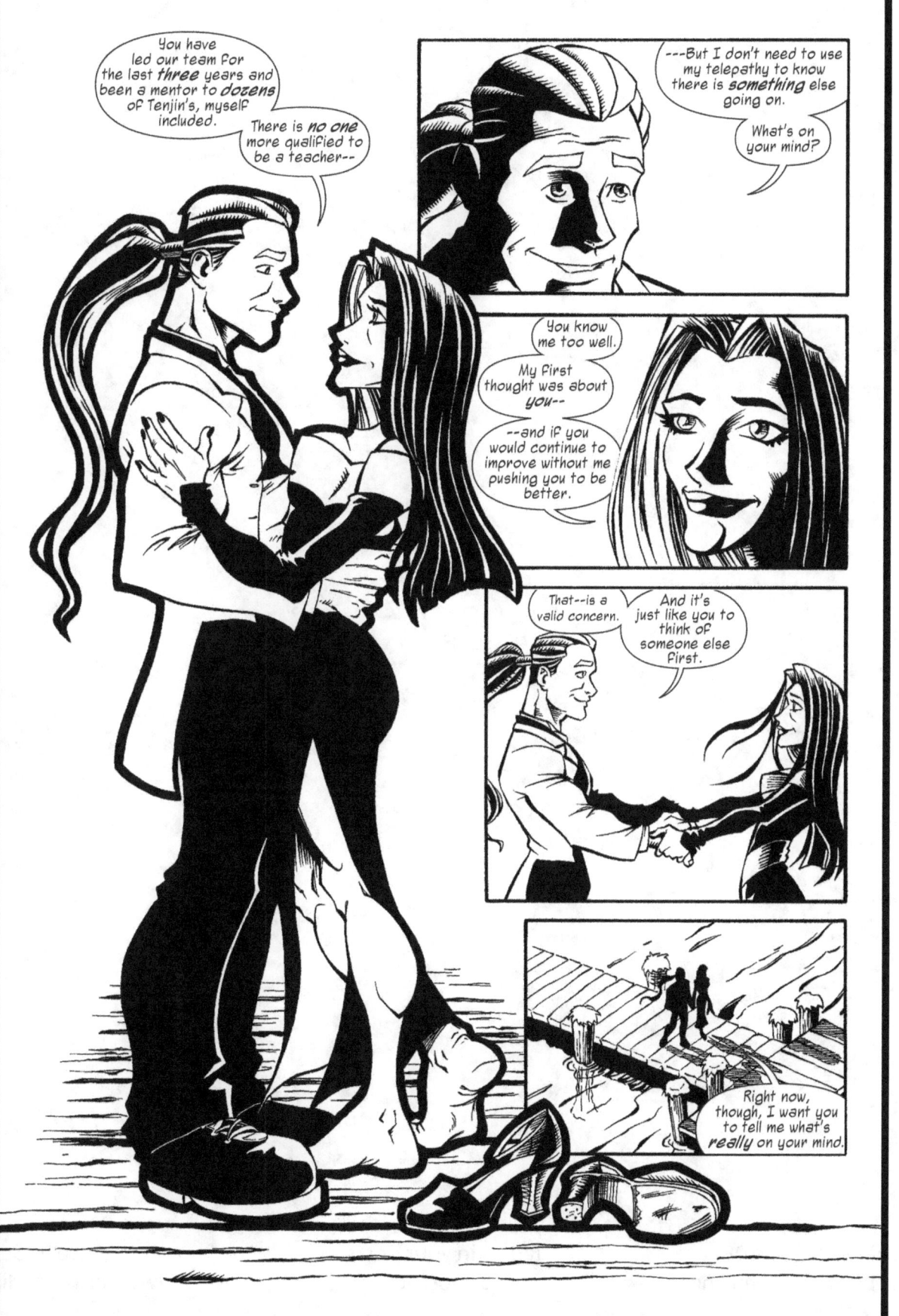

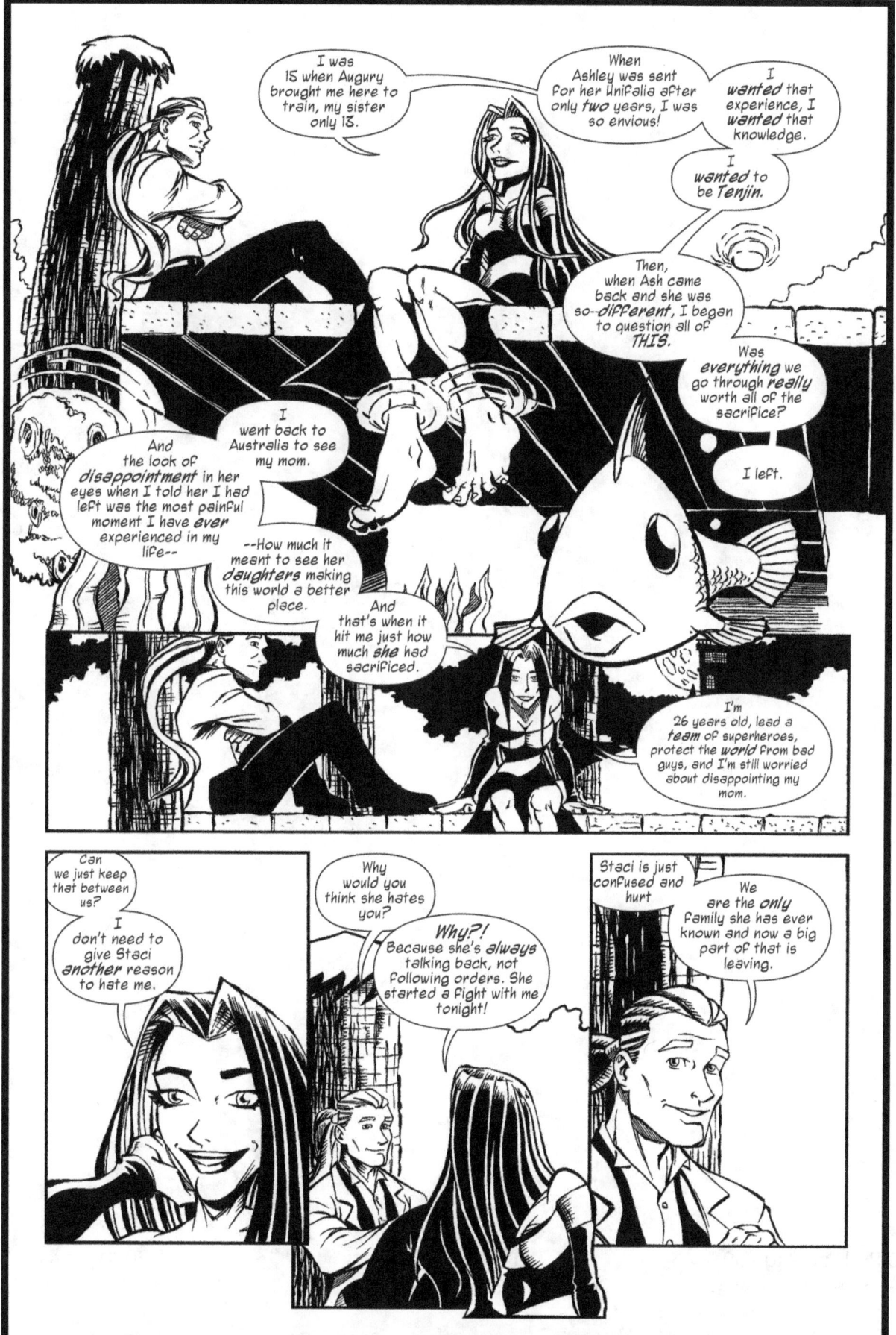

Shinjū Prelude Page 09
Lineart by Erich Owen and
Travis Stephens

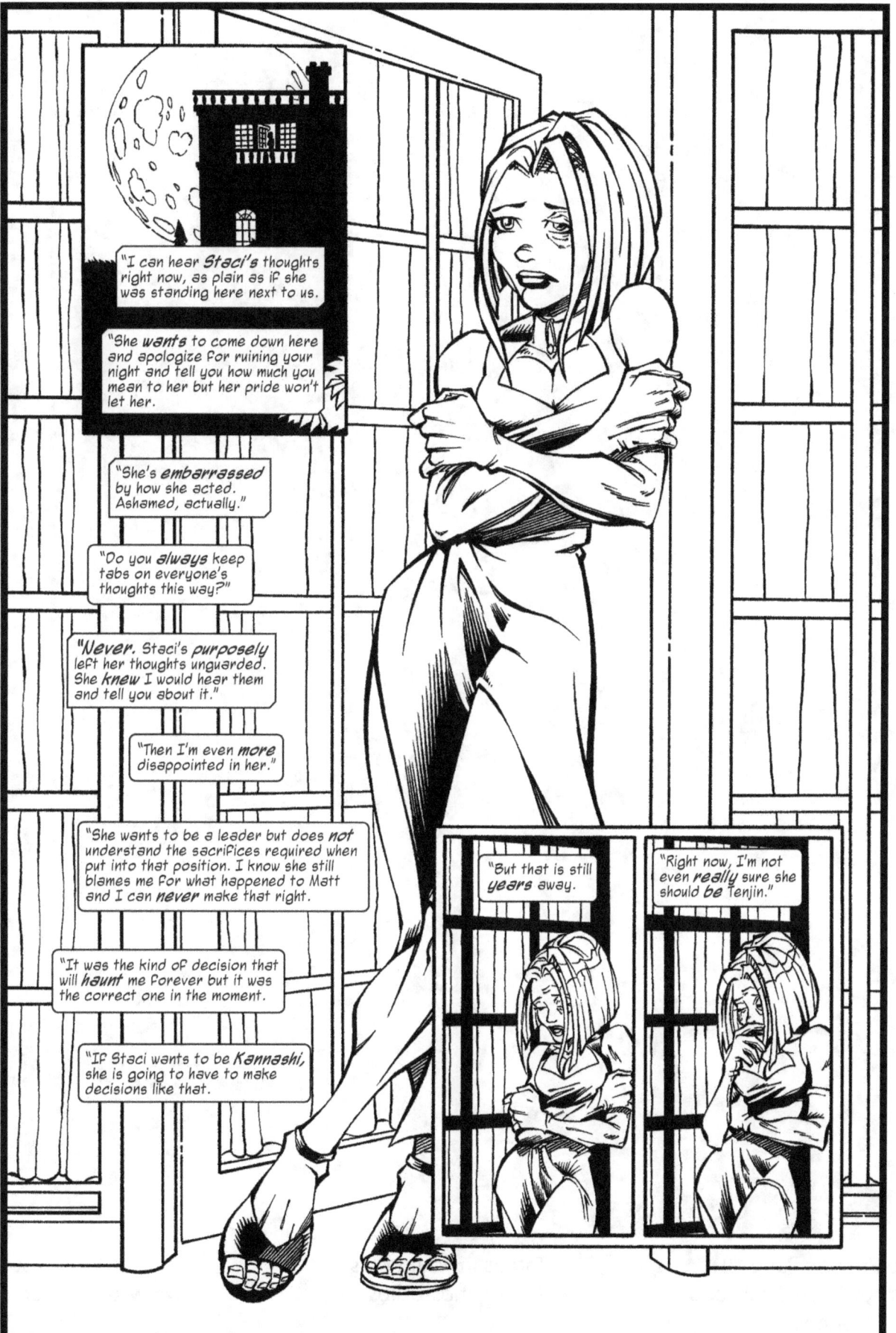

Shinjū Prelude Page 10
Lineart by Erich Owen and
Travis Stephens

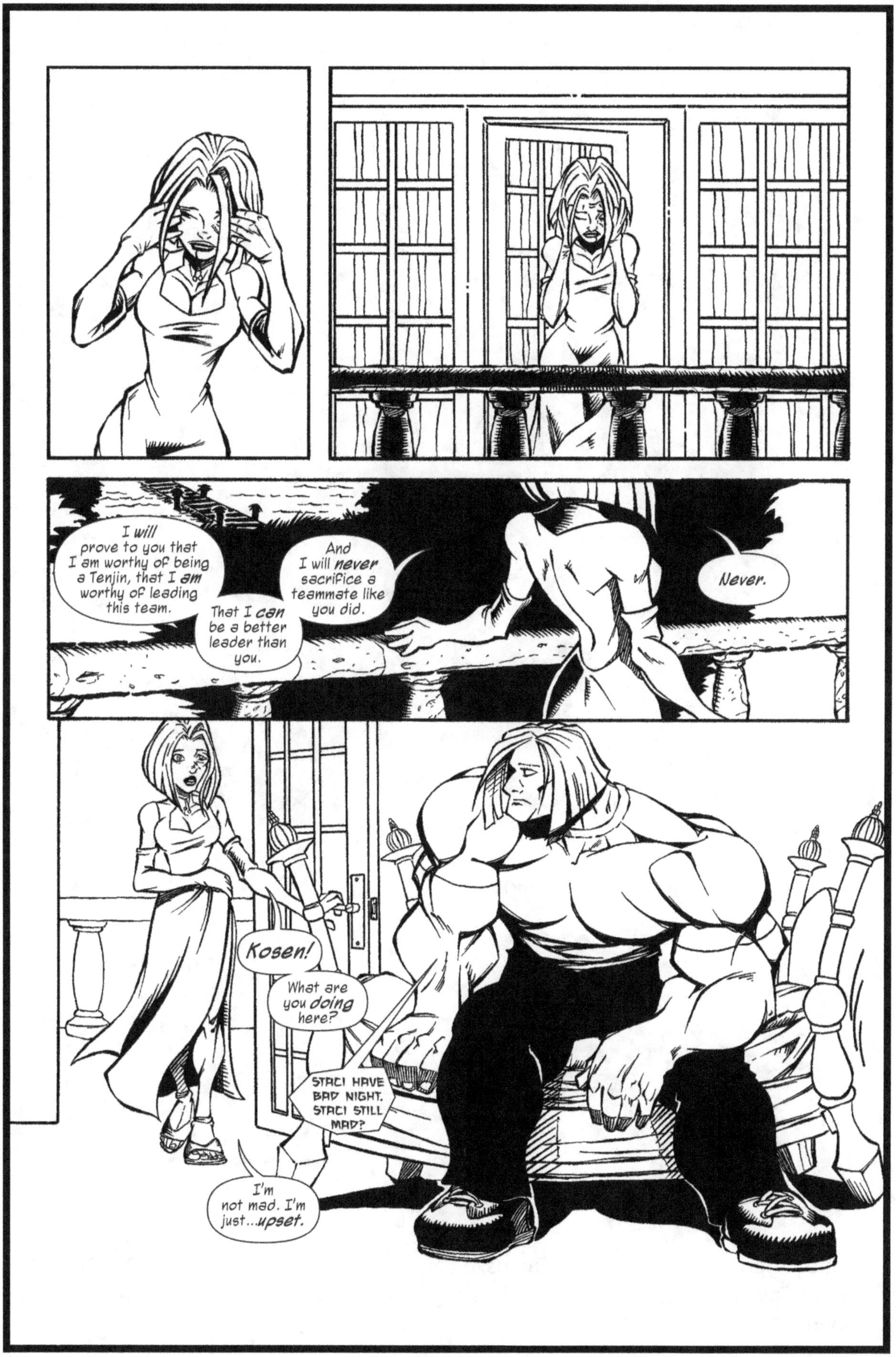

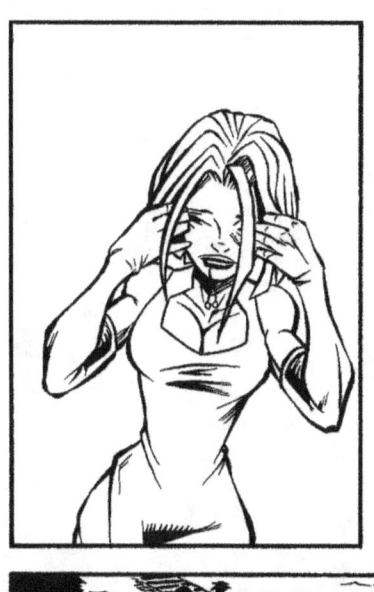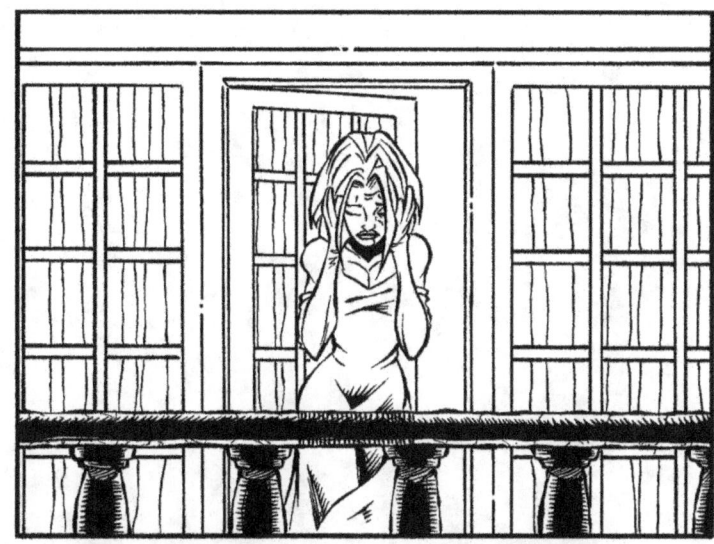

Shinjū Prelude Page 11
Lineart by Erich Owen and
Travis Stephens

© 2020 Travis Stephens
www.kaishostudios.com

Tag us in your posts!
@kaishostudios

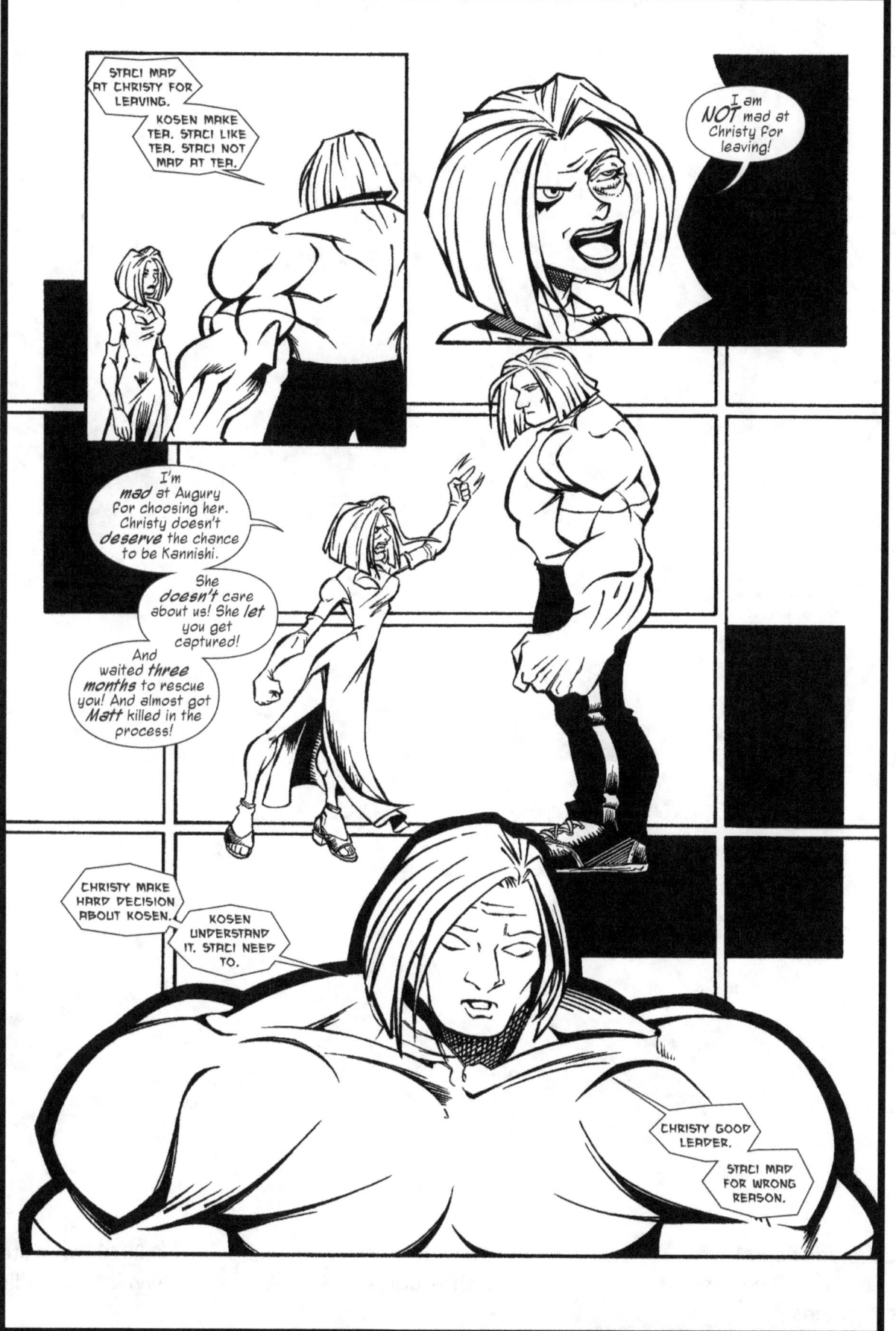

Shinjū Prelude Page 12
Lineart by Erich Owen and Travis Stephens

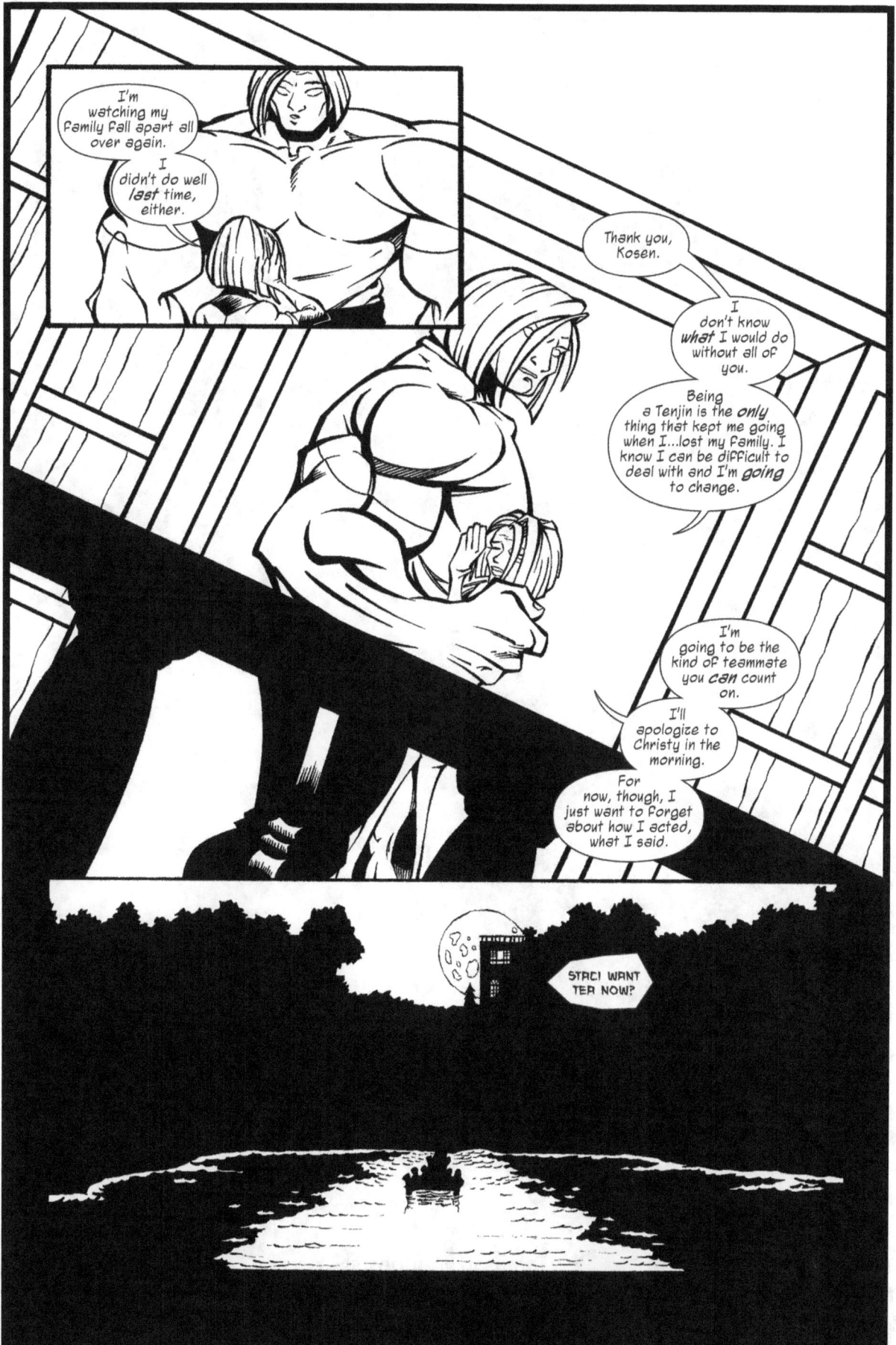

Shinjū Prelude Page 13
Lineart by Erich Owen and
Travis Stephens

Tag us in your posts!
@kaishostudios

© 2020 Travis Stephens
www.kaishostudios.com

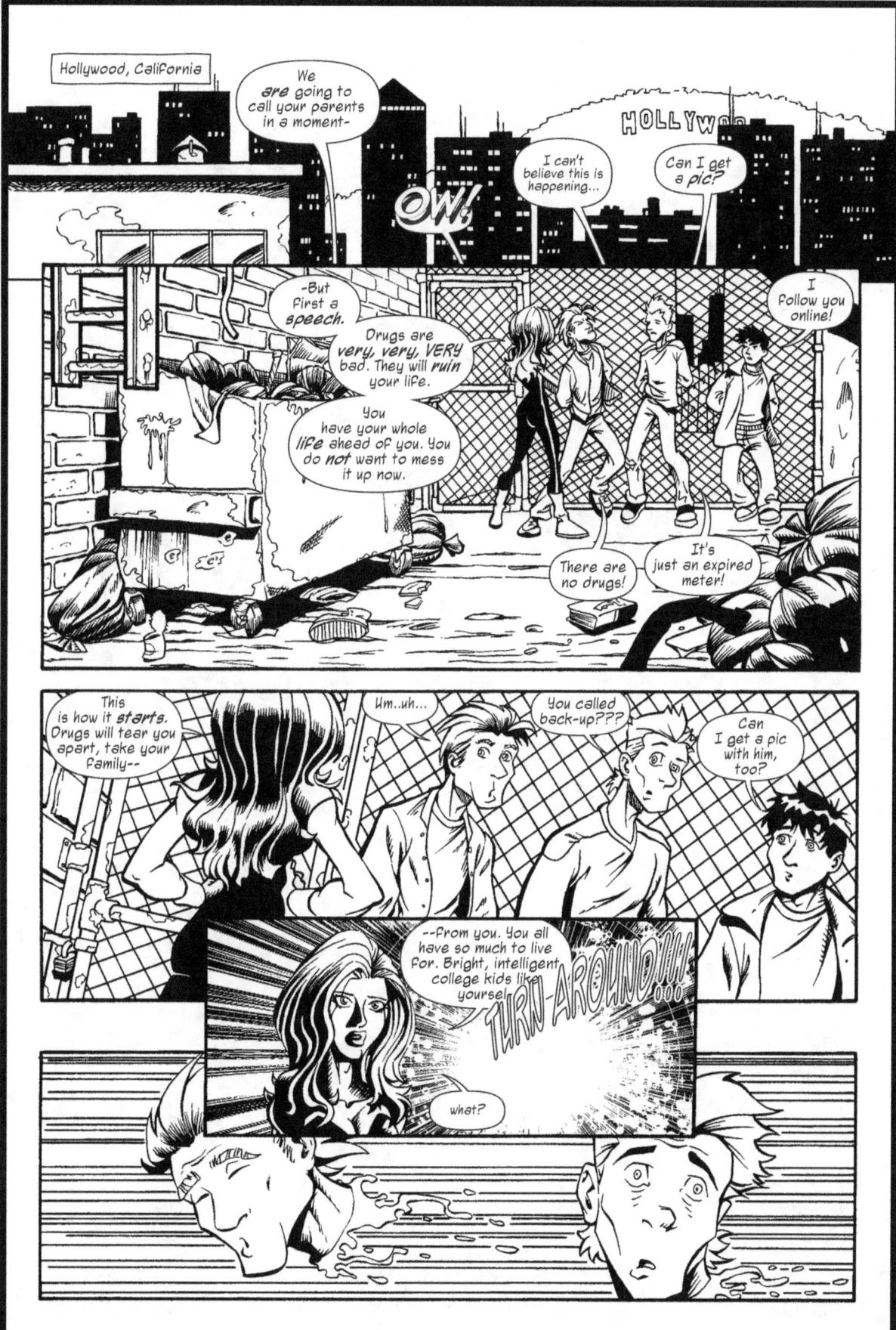

Shinjū Prelude Page 14
Lineart by Erich Owen and
Travis Stephens

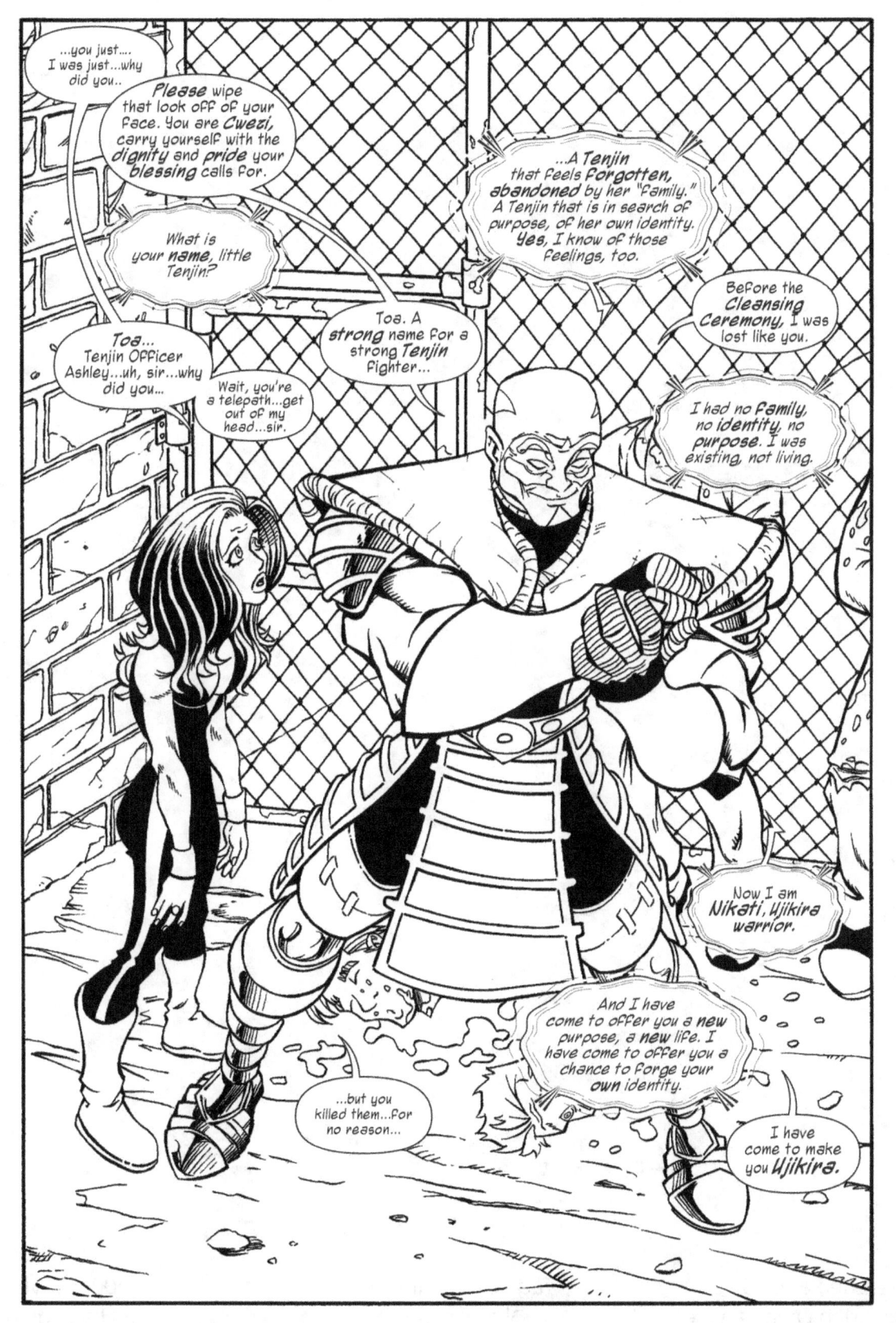

Shinjū Prelude Page 15
Lineart by Erich Owen and
Travis Stephens

© 2020 Travis Stephens
www.kaishostudios.com

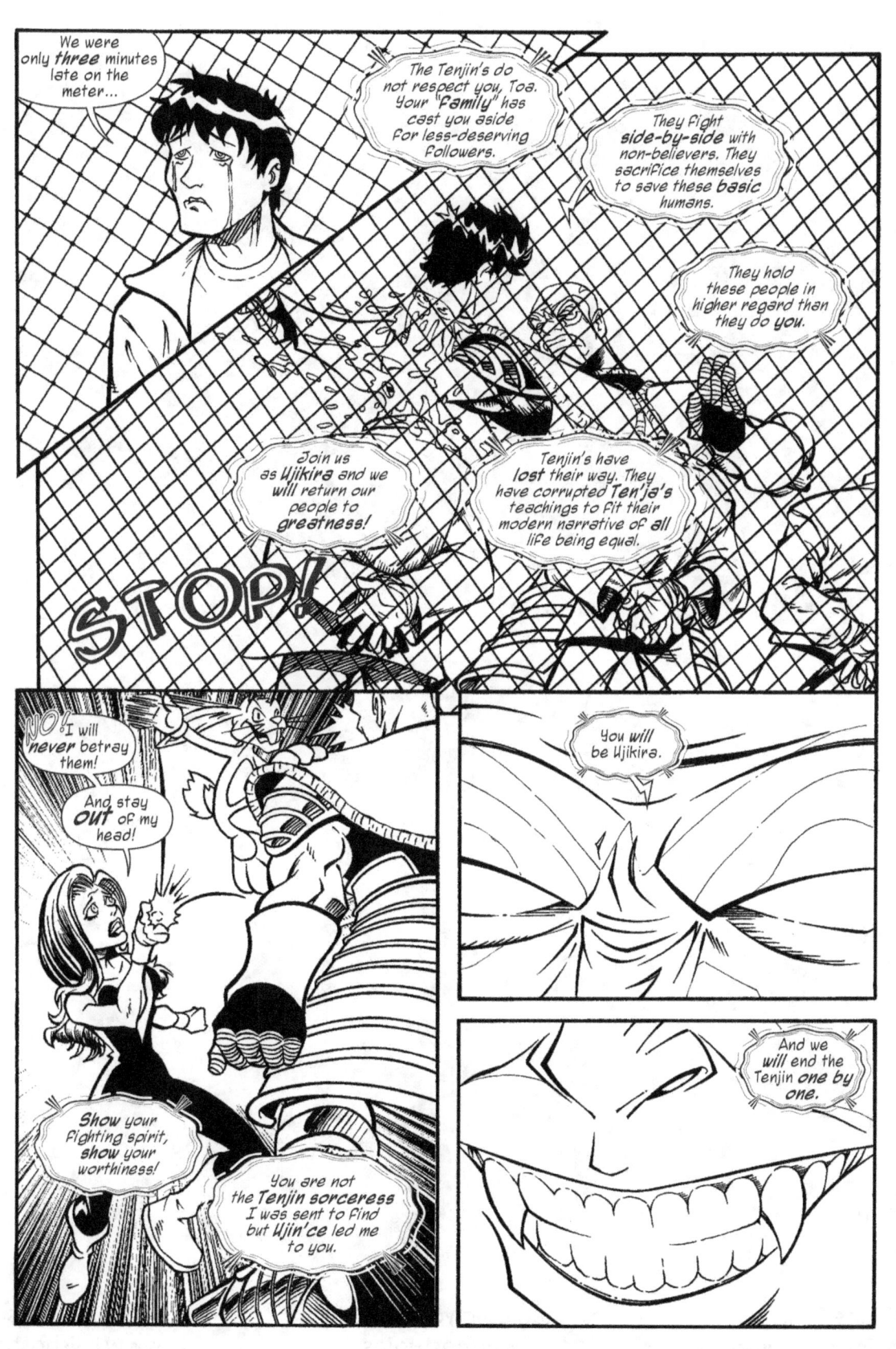

Shinjū Prelude Page 16
Lineart by Erich Owen and Travis Stephens

Tag us in your posts!
@kaishostudios

© 2020 Travis Stephens
www.kaishostudios.com

Pacific Estate, Crawford, Colorado

"Christy, you *can* teleport into town. The teleporters would *gladly* do it for you."

"After all they did during the *Scourge invasion,* they need the rest."

"If *anything* comes up, they can lock onto my position and have me back here in *sixty* seconds."

"You just want to stick your hand out of the window and sing terrible *80's* songs."

"*Joseph!* Stop reading my thoughts!"

"*"Nothin' But A Good Time"* is a classic. Bret Michaels spoke to a generation with his lyrics..."

WHOA!

"Calm down, Tiger. I'm not reading your thoughts."

"You *better* not be. It'll ruin tonight's surprise if you are."

"I'm friggin' hungry!"

"Just walk down the stairs!"

"I need ₯₯₯₯₯₯"

"You can do it!"

"Is Ashley still meeting up with you guys?"

"I hope so. I owe her a high five for what she did during the Invasion."

"Joseph..."

"Yay!!! Just a few more steps!"

"You are awesome!"

"Big breakfast platter!"

"A "high five?" Not a hug?"

"She's not big on hugging. Or displays of affection. Or praise."

"We're a *complicated* family, OK?"

"I'll see you when I get back--"

"--with your surprise."

"Joseph..."

"I can't wait."

"Joseph..."

"≷sigh≷ Our Chizan is calling me."

"Be safe and call if anything happens."

Shinjū Prelude Page 17
Lineart by Erich Owen and
Travis Stephens

© 2020 Travis Stephens
www.kaishostudios.com

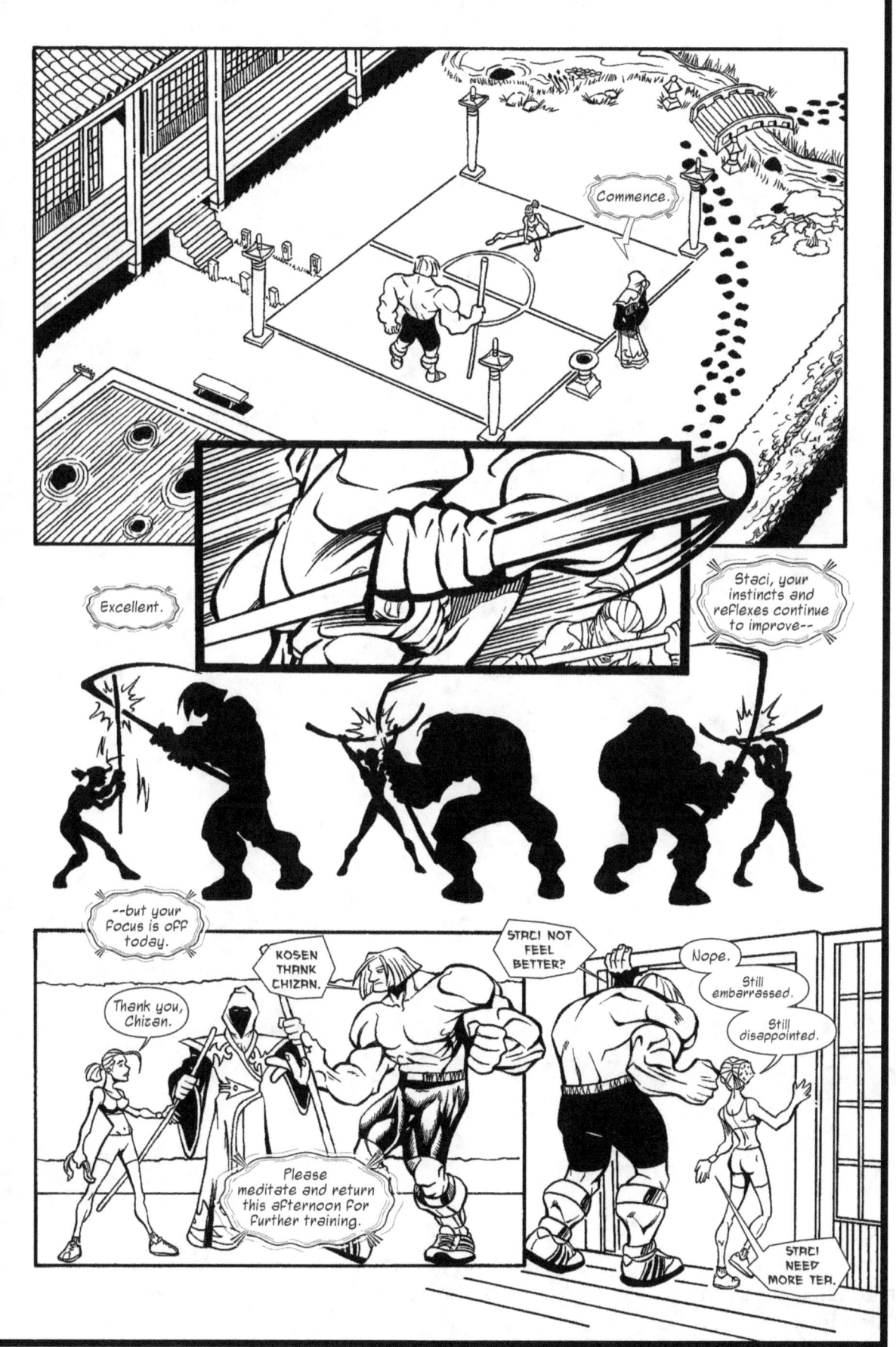

Shinjū Prelude Page 18
Lineart by Erich Owen and
Travis Stephens

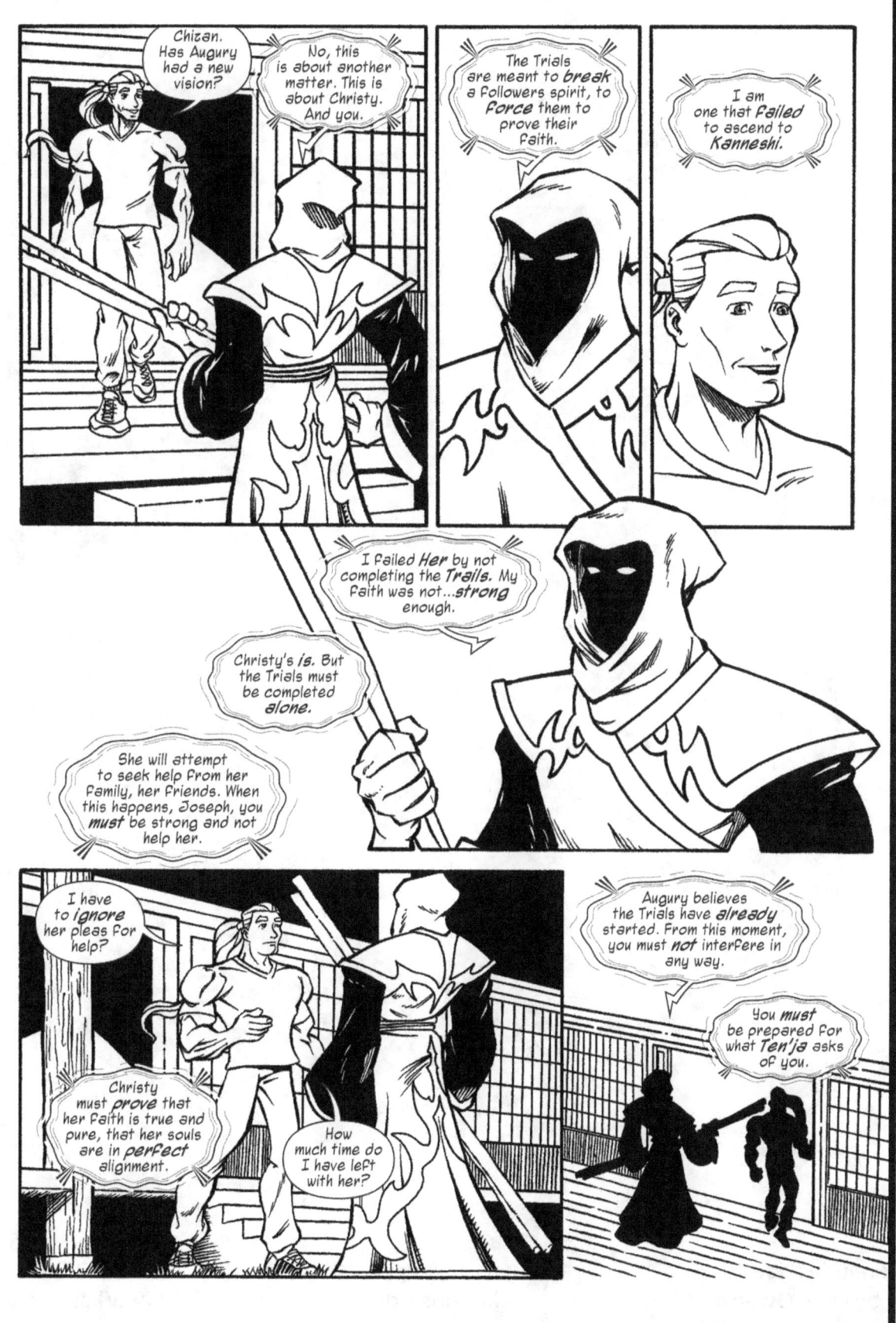

Shinjū Prelude Page 19
Lineart by Erich Owen and
Travis Stephens

© 2020 Travis Stephens
www.kaishostudios.com

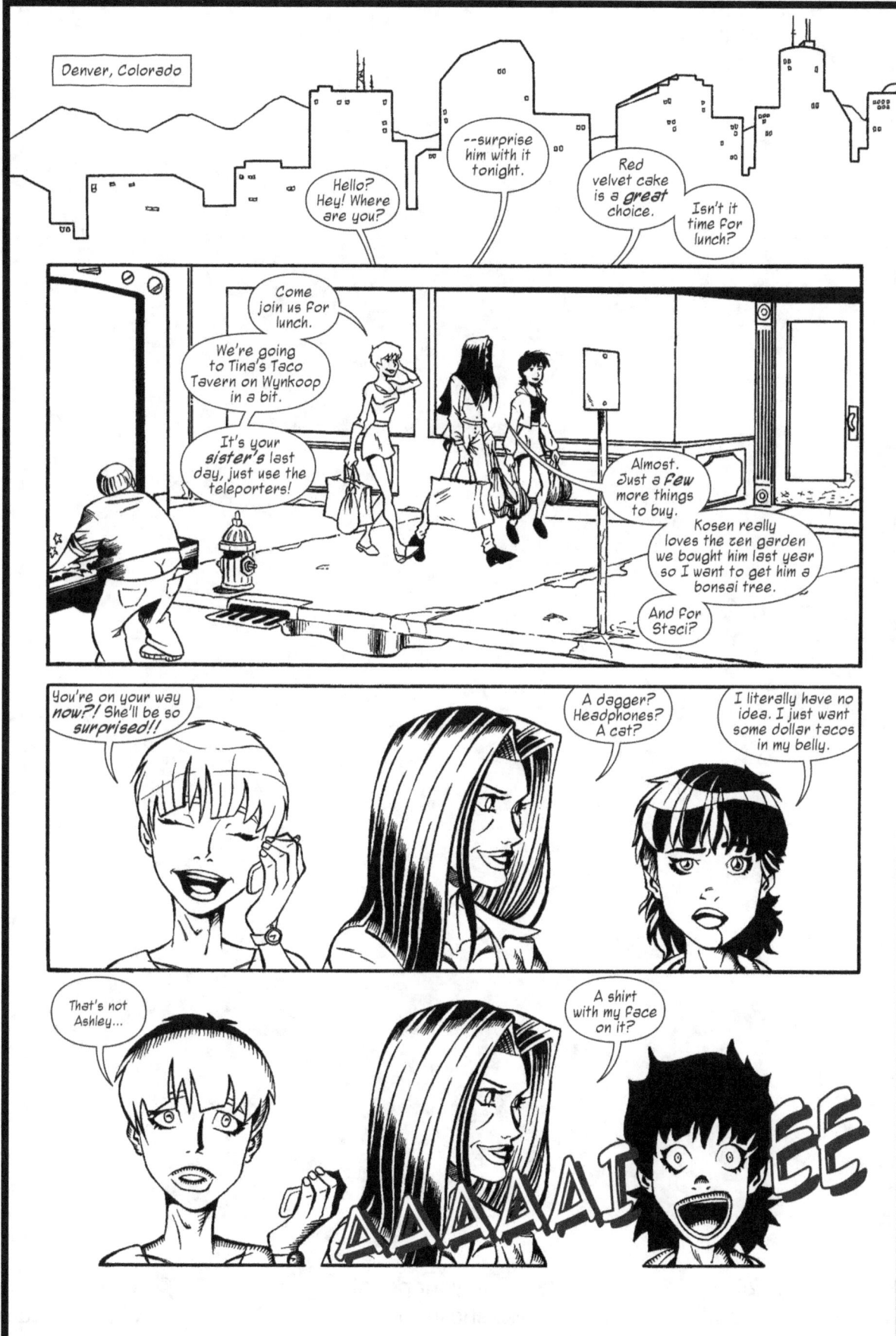

Shinjū Prelude Page 20
Lineart by Erich Owen and Travis Stephens

Tag us in your posts!
@kaishostudios

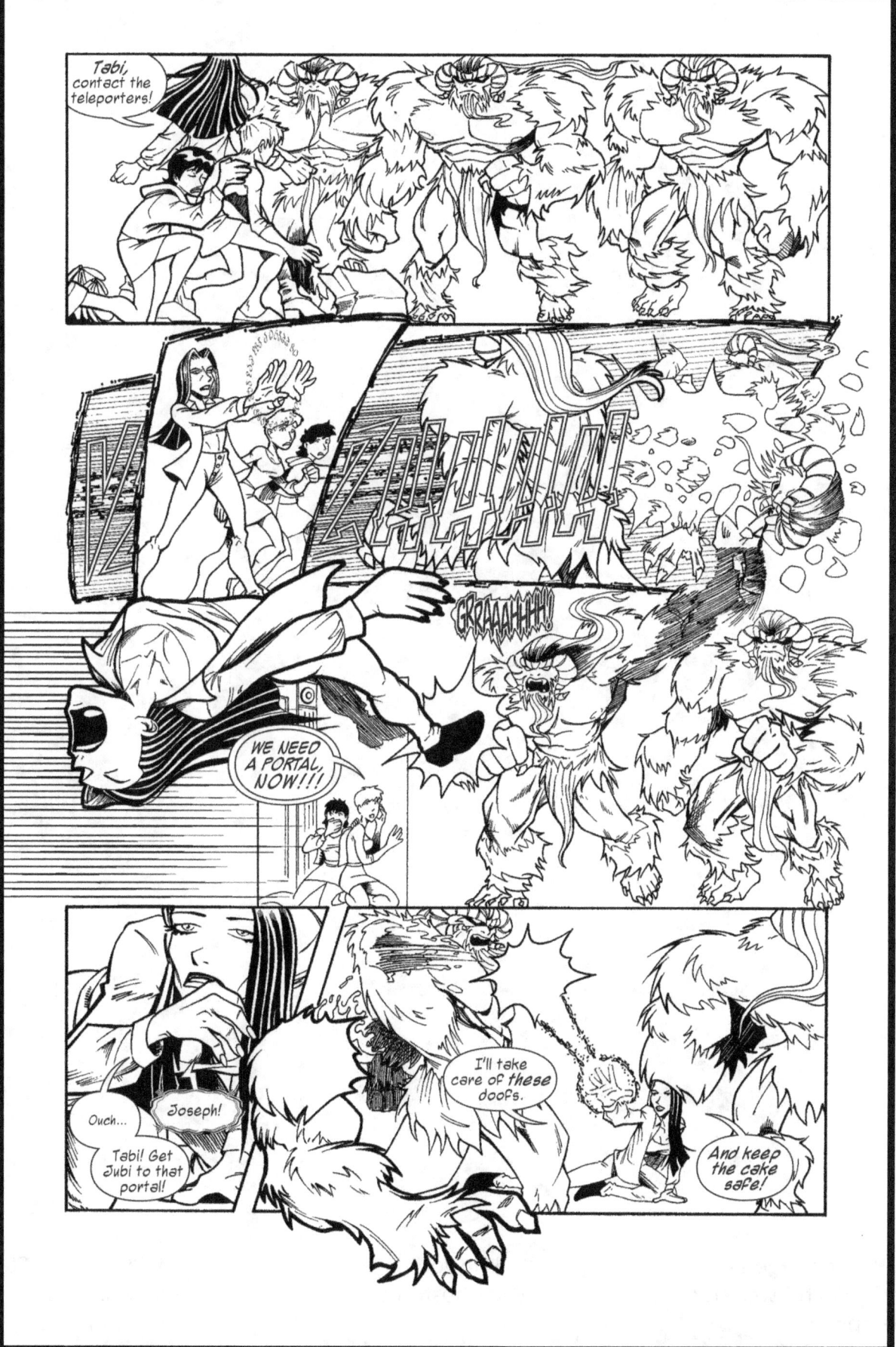

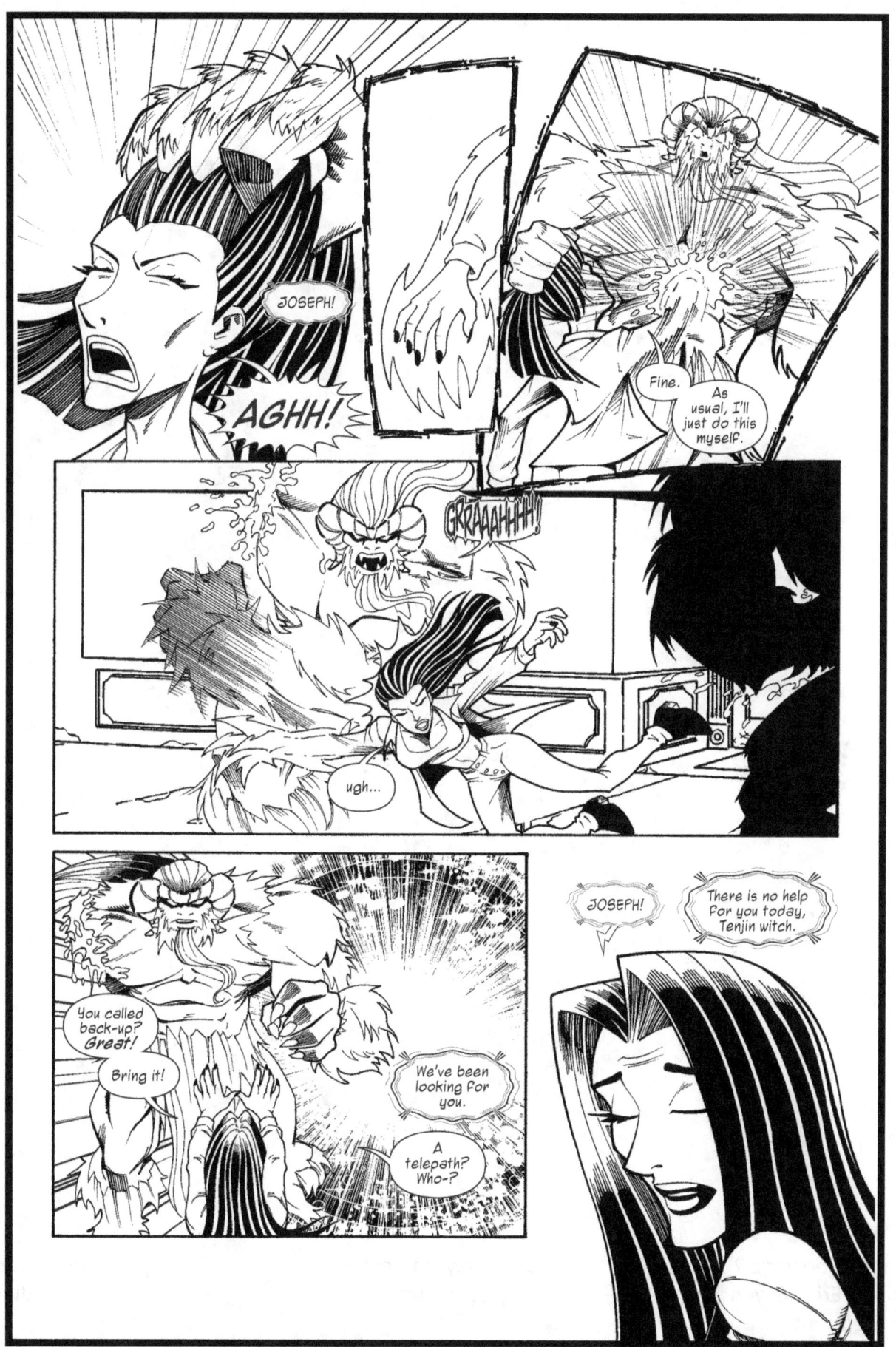

Shinjū Prelude Page 22
Lineart by Erich Owen and Travis Stephens

Tag us in your posts!
@kaishostudios

© 2020 Travis Stephens
www.kaishostudios.com

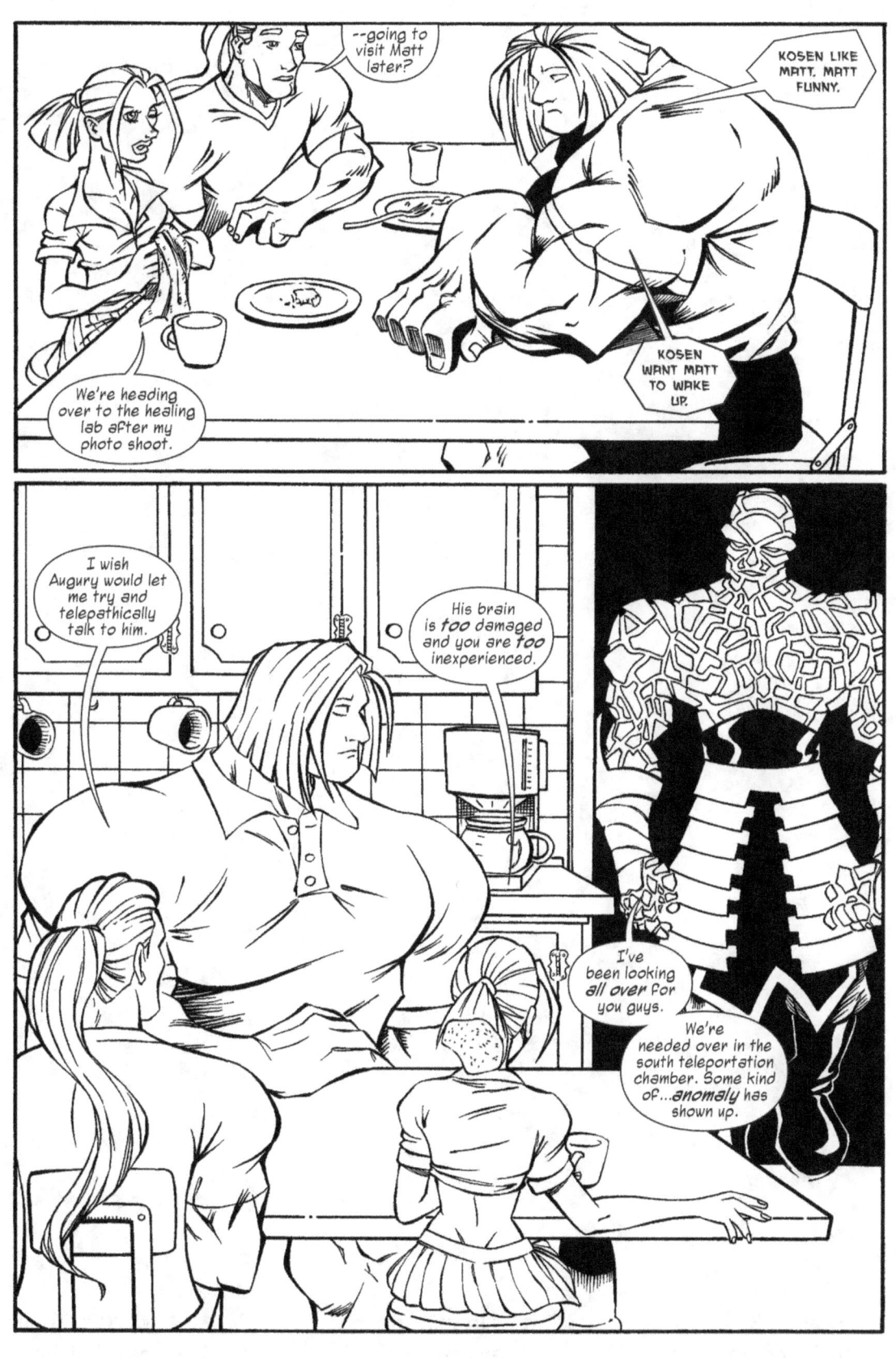

Shinjū Prelude Page 23
Lineart by Erich Owen and
Travis Stephens

Tag us in your posts!
@kaishostudios

© 2020 Travis Stephens
www.kaishostudios.com

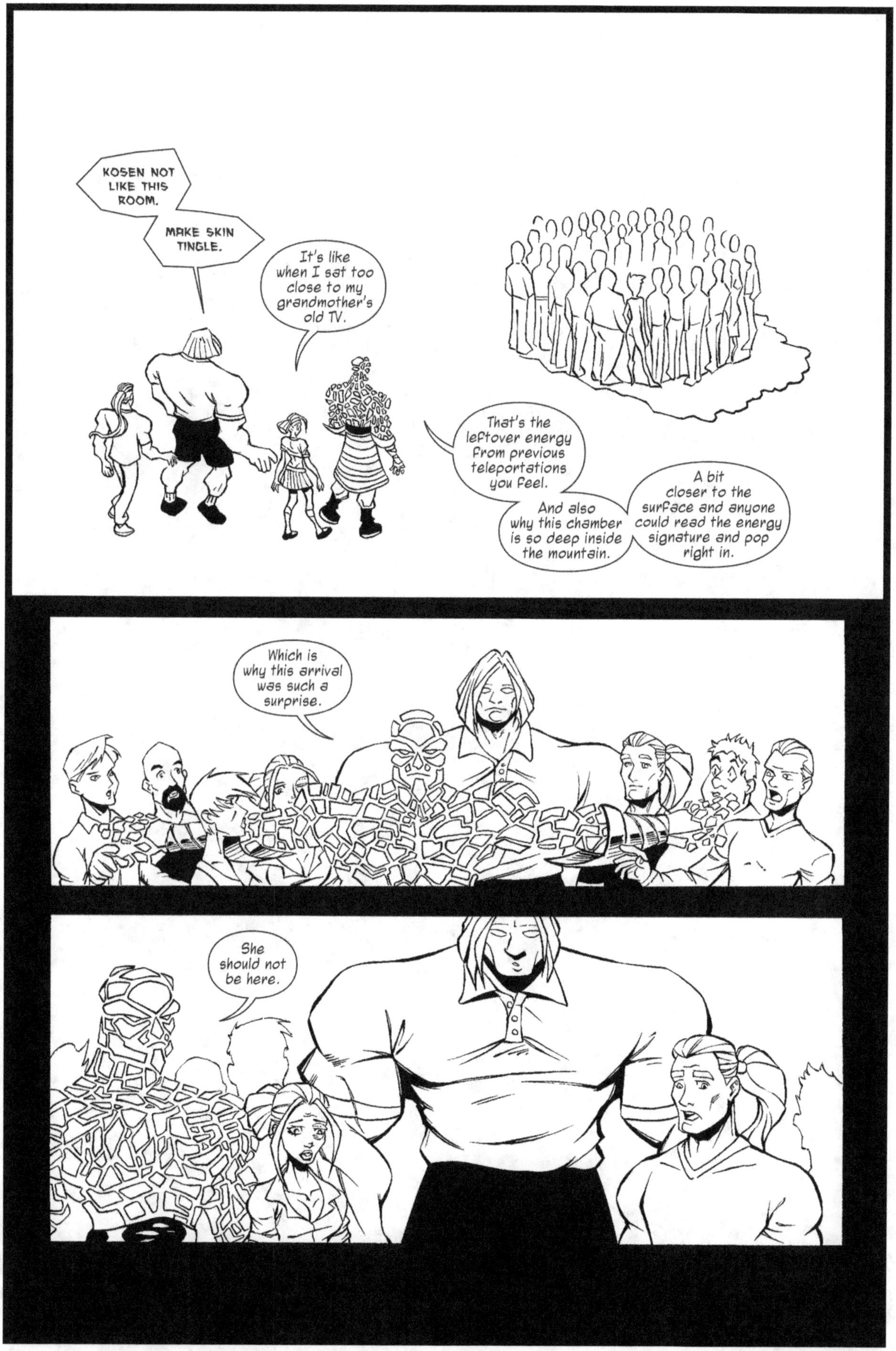

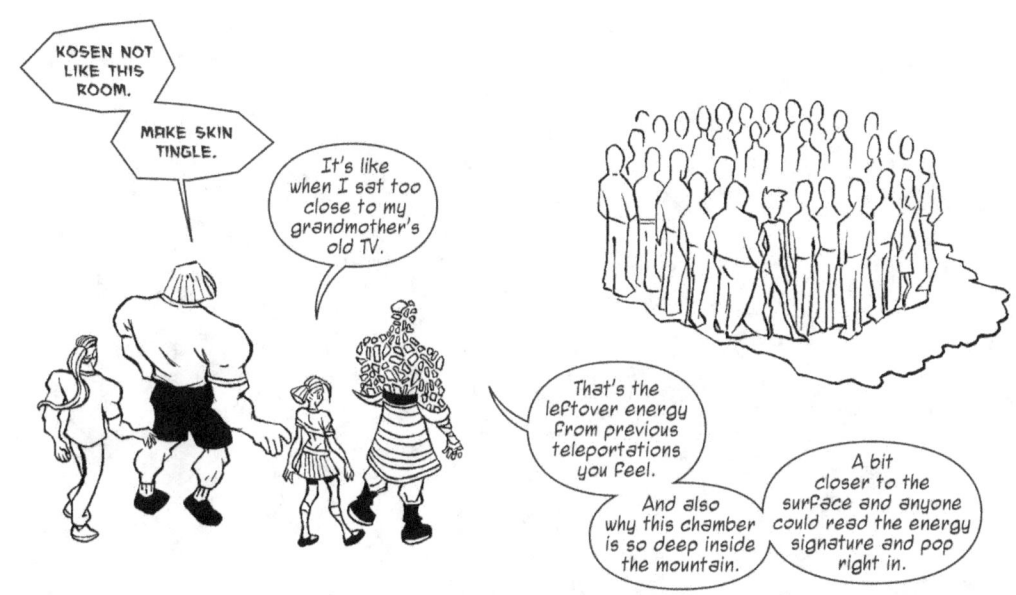

Shinjū Prelude Page 24
Lineart by Erich Owen and Travis Stephens

Tag us in your posts!
@kaishostudios

© 2020 Travis Stephens
www.kaishostudios.com

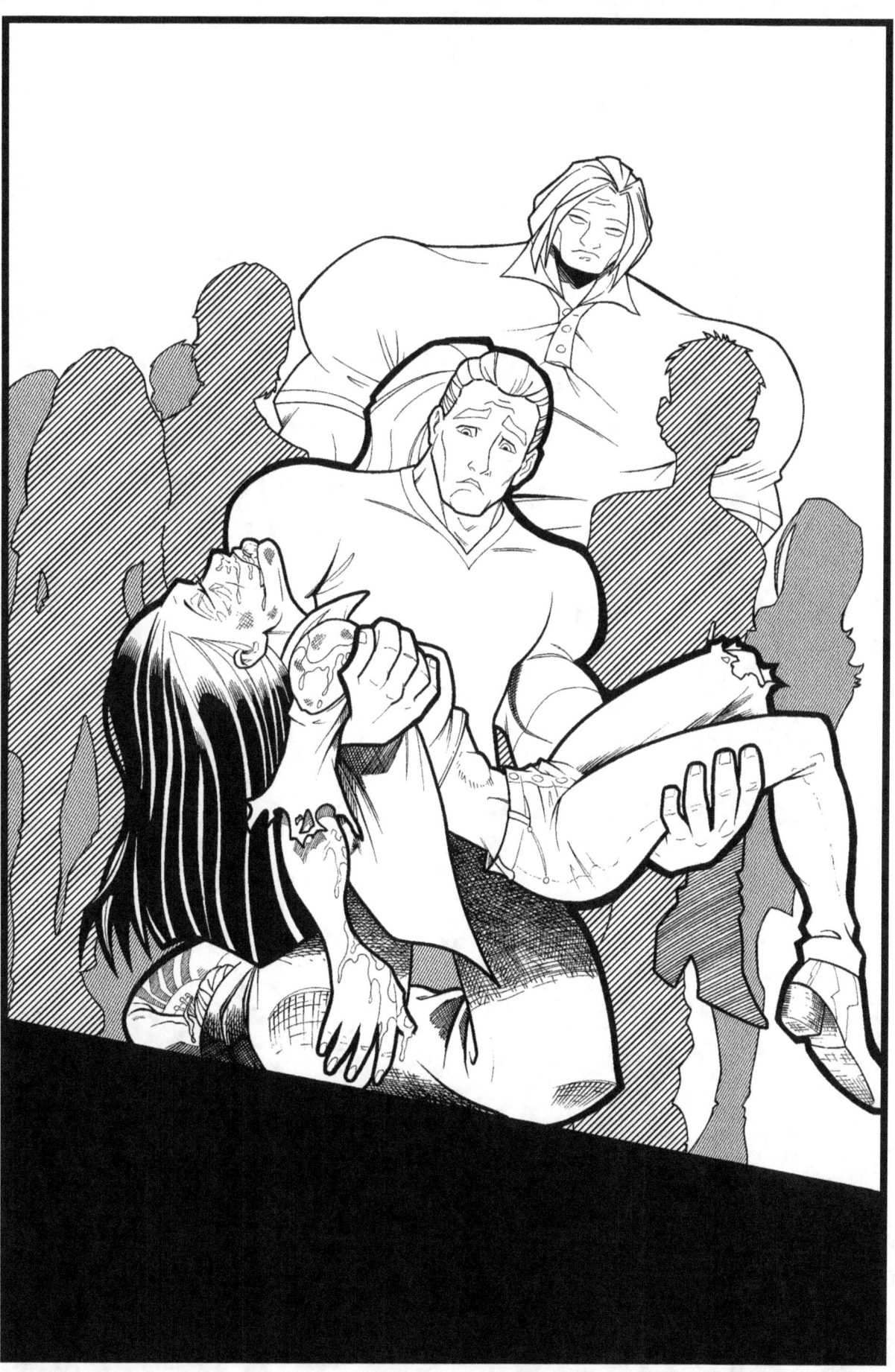

Shinjū Prelude Page 25
Lineart by Erich Owen and
Travis Stephens

Tag us in your posts!
@kaishostudios

© 2020 Travis Stephens
www.kaishostudios.com

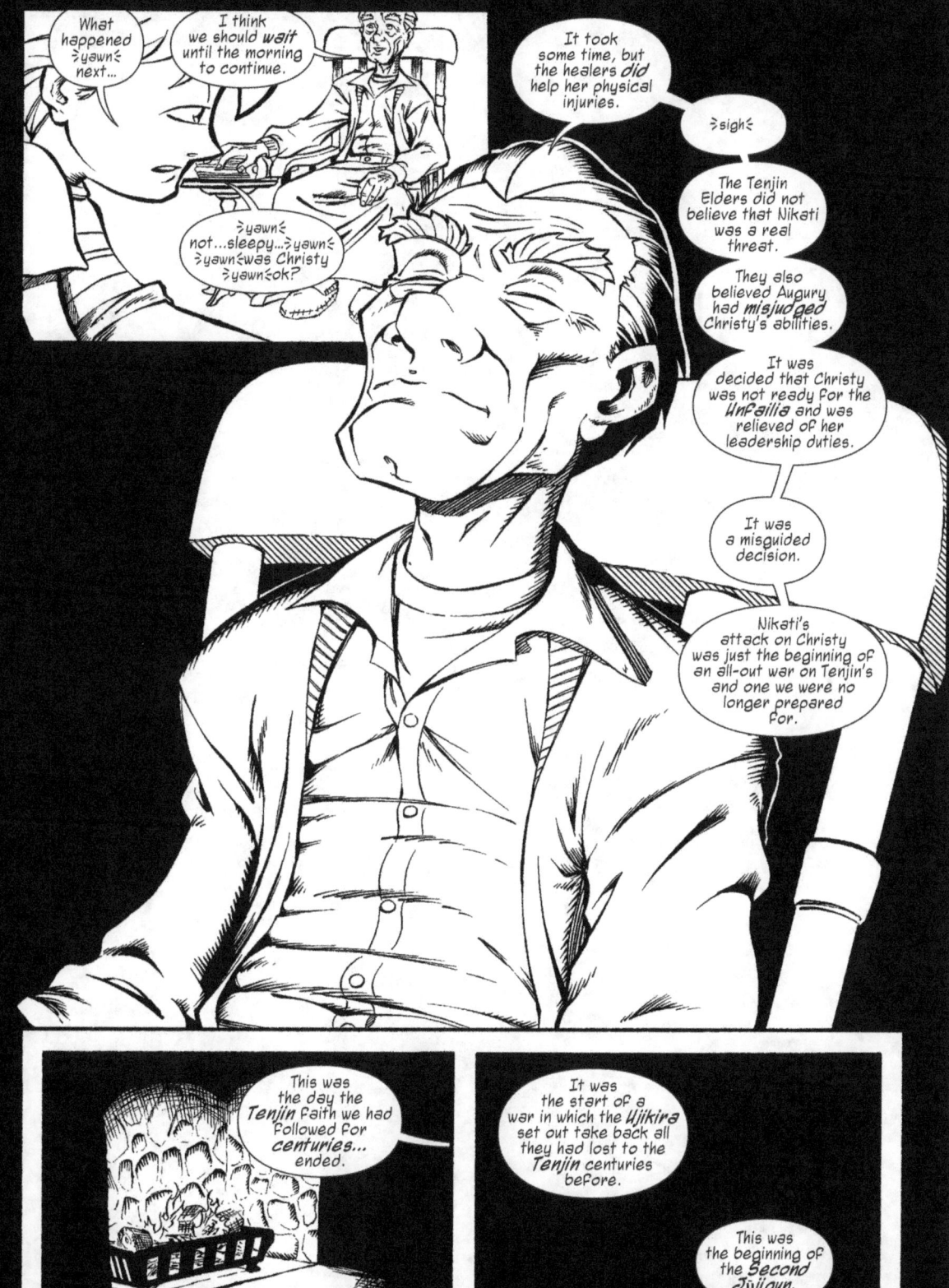

Shinjū Prelude Page 26
Lineart by Erich Owen and Travis Stephens

Tag us in your posts!
@kaishostudios

© 2020 Travis Stephens
www.kaishostudios.com

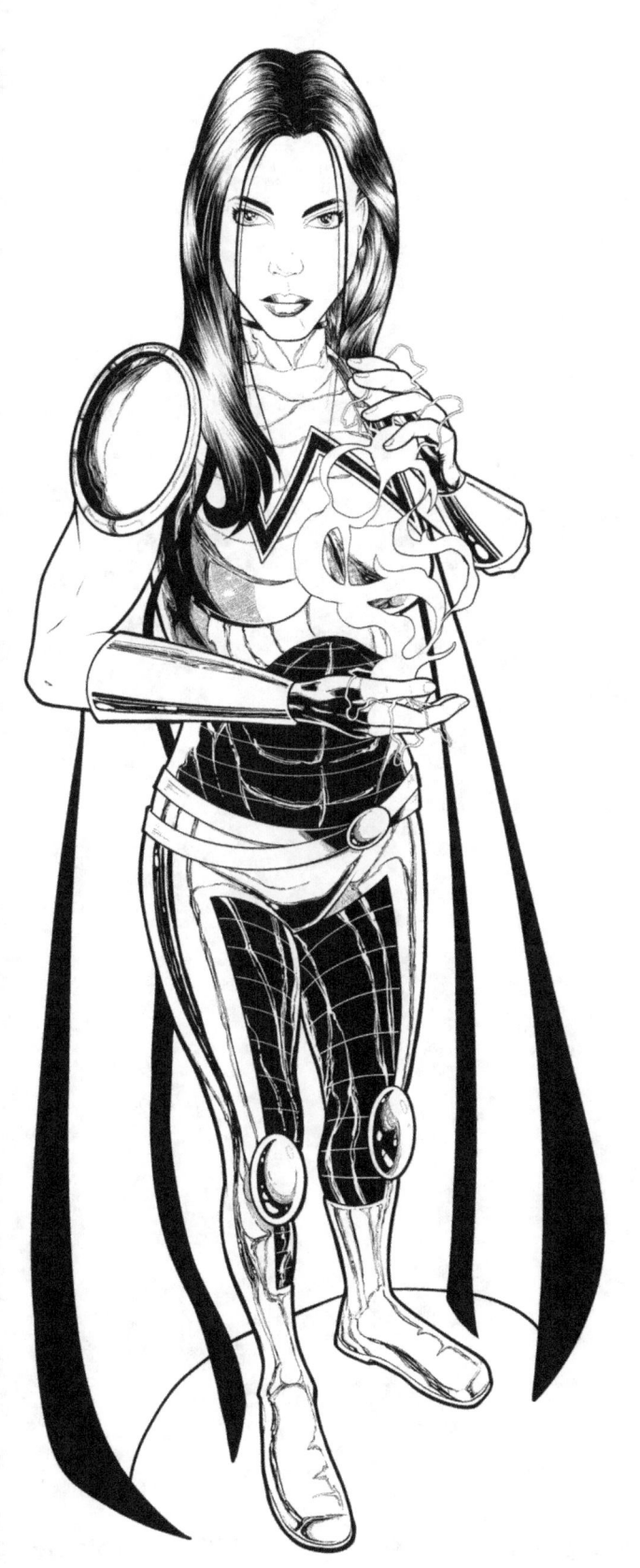

Christy Anders

-BIOGRAPHICAL DATA-
REAL NAME: Christy Anders
PLACE OF BIRTH: Perth, Western Australia, Australia
Age: 28
MARITAL STATUS: Single
KNOWN RELATIVES: Ashley Anders (sister); Unnamed mother
KNOWN CONFIDANTS: Joseph Raider
BASE OF OPERATIONS: Pacific Estate, Crawford, Colorado
CURRENT GROUP MEMBERSHIP: The Tenjin

-PHYSICAL DESCRIPTION-
HEIGHT: 6'1"
WEIGHT: 160 lbs.
EYES: Green
HAIR: Black; Dyed purple currently
OTHER DISTINGUISHING FEATURES: Rose tattoo on her left shoulder blade

-POWERS AND ABILITIES-
STRENGTH: Normal
SPECIAL SKILLS AND ABILITIES: Fluent in ancient Tenjin
SUPERHUMAN PHYSICAL POWERS: None
SUPERHUMAN MENTAL POWERS: Sorcerey
SPECIAL LIMITATIONS: Spells must be memorized
SOURCE OF SUPERHUMAN POWERS: Divine gift from Ten'ja

Shinjū Prelude Christy Anders
Lineart by Travis Stephens

Tag us in your posts!
@kaishostudios

© 2020 Travis Stephens
www.kaishostudios.com

Joseph Raider

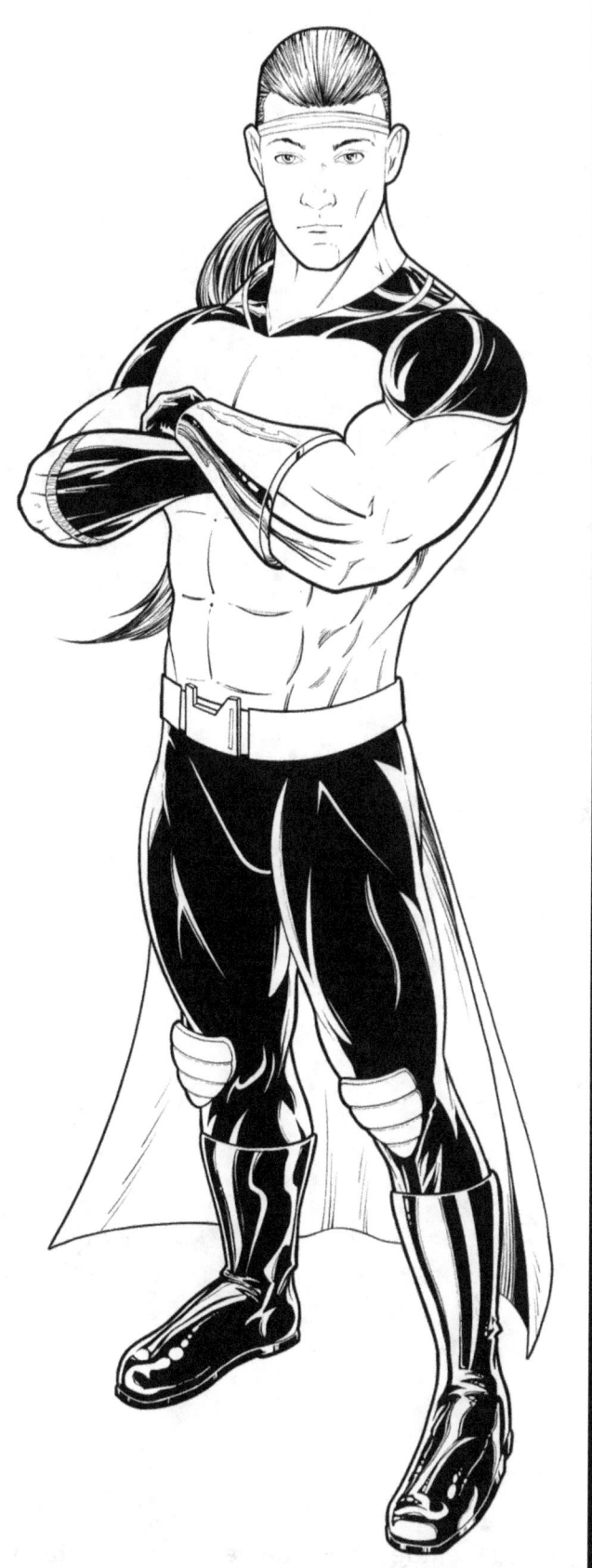

-BIOGRAPHICAL DATA-
REAL NAME: Joseph Raider
PLACE OF BIRTH: Alabaster, Alabama
AGE: 22
MARITAL STATUS: Single
KNOWN RELATIVES: None known
KNOWN CONFIDANTS: Christy Anders
BASE OF OPERATIONS: Pacific Estate, Crawford, Colorado
CURRENT GROUP MEMBERSHIP: The Tenjin

-PHYSICAL DESCRIPTION-
HEIGHT: 6'0"
WEIGHT: 220 lbs.
EYES: Blue
HAIR: Brown
OTHER DISTINGUISHING FEATURES: None

-POWERS AND ABILITIES-
STRENGTH: Superhuman
SPECIAL SKILLS AND ABILITIES: None
SUPERHUMAN PHYSICAL POWERS: None
SUPERHUMAN MENTAL POWERS: Telepathy and telekinesis
SPECIAL LIMITATIONS: Telekinetic powers are still developing
SOURCE OF SUPERHUMAN POWERS: Divine gift from Ten'ja

Shinjū Prelude Joseph Raider
Lineart by Travis Stephens

Tag us in your posts!
@kaishostudios

© 2020 Travis Stephens
www.kaishostudios.com

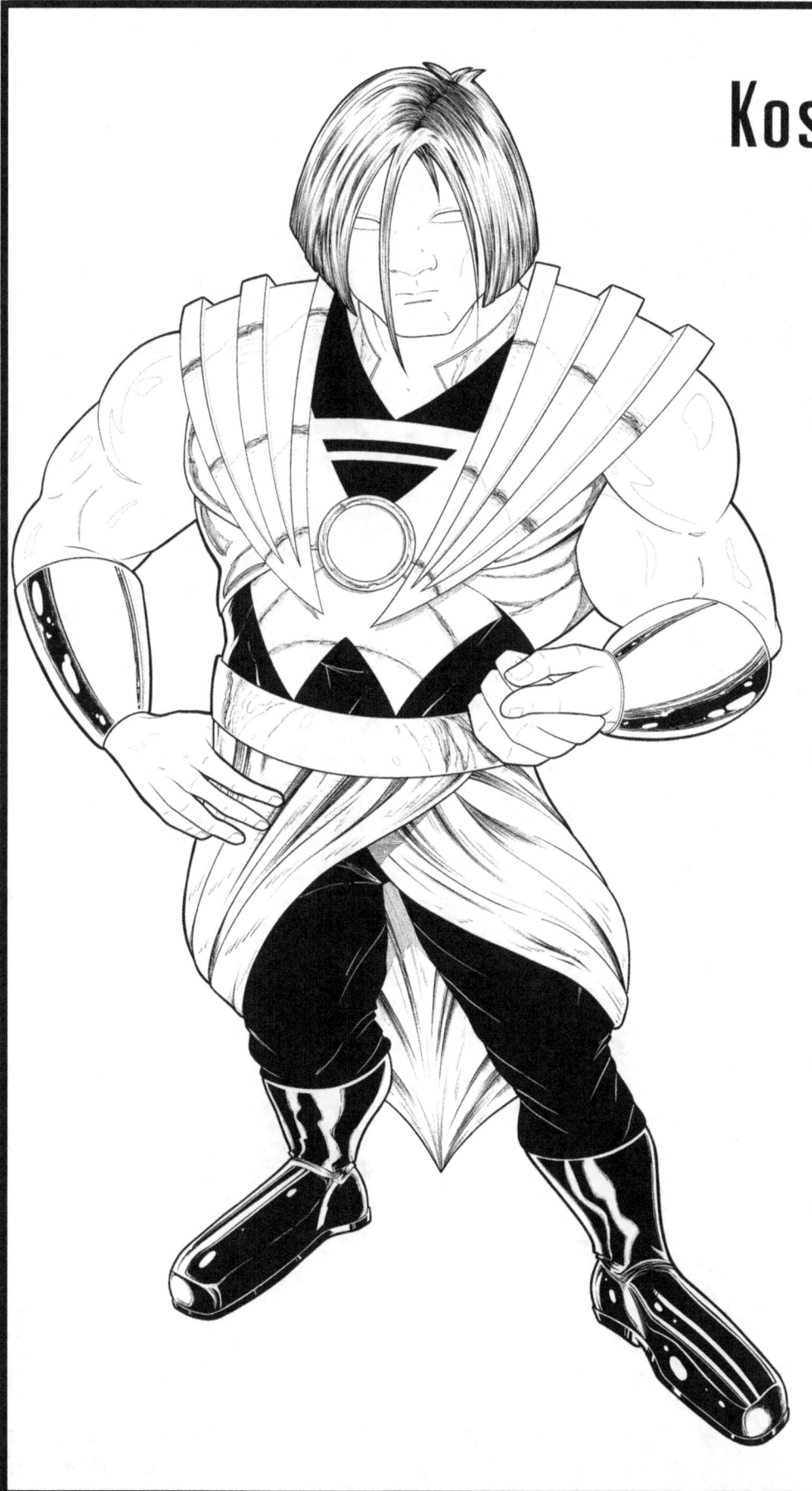

Kosen

-BIOGRAPHICAL DATA-
REAL NAME: Unknown
PLACE OF BIRTH: Unknown
AGE: Unknown
MARITAL STATUS: Single
KNOWN RELATIVES: None known
KNOWN CONFIDANTS: Staci Brigitte
BASE OF OPERATIONS: Pacific Estate, Crawford, Colorado
CURRENT GROUP MEMBERSHIP: The Tenjin

-PHYSICAL DESCRIPTION-
HEIGHT: 7'1"
WEIGHT: 350 lbs.
EYES: White
HAIR: None
OTHER DISTINGUISHING FEATURES: Skin is reflective

-POWERS AND ABILITIES-
STRENGTH: Superhuman
SPECIAL SKILLS AND ABILITIES: Fluent in ancient Tenjin
SUPERHUMAN PHYSICAL POWERS: Strength
SUPERHUMAN MENTAL POWERS: Light manipulation
SPECIAL LIMITATIONS: Kosen needs ultraviolet light to survive
SOURCE OF SUPERHUMAN POWERS: Tenjin Unifailia Ceremony

Shinjū Prelude Kosen
Lineart by Travis Stephens

Tag us in your posts!
@kaishostudios

© 2020 Travis Stephens
www.kaishostudios.com

Rad

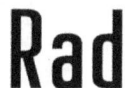

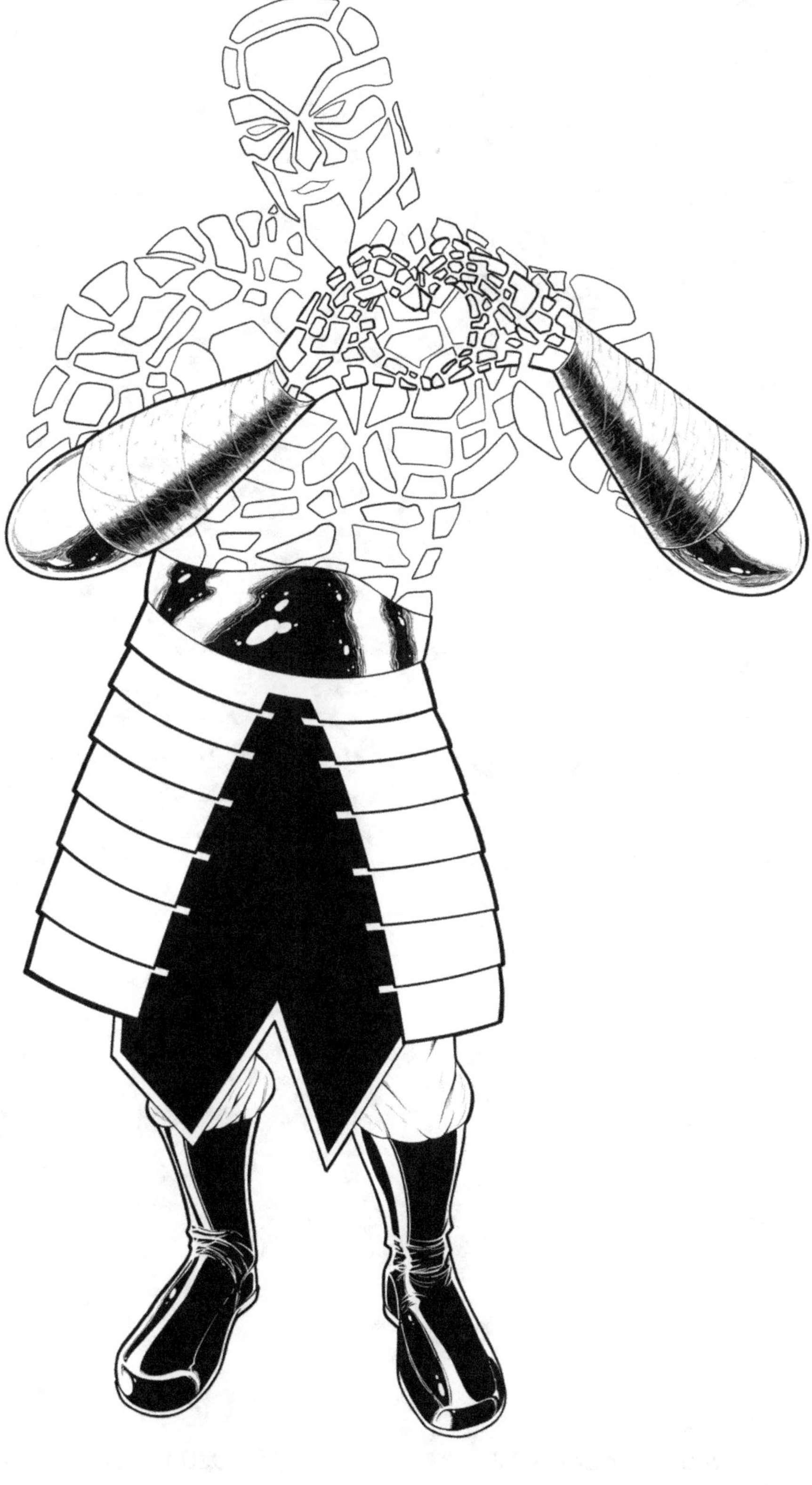

-BIOGRAPHICAL DATA-
REAL NAME: Miku Kikuchi
PLACE OF BIRTH: Shinshiro, Aichi Prefecture, Japan
Age: 30
MARITAL STATUS: Single
KNOWN RELATIVES: None known
KNOWN CONFIDANTS: Joseph Raider
BASE OF OPERATIONS: Pacific Estate, Crawford, Colorado
CURRENT GROUP MEMBERSHIP: The Tenjin

-PHYSICAL DESCRIPTION-
HEIGHT: 5'6"
WEIGHT: 400 lbs.
EYES: Yellow
HAIR: None
OTHER DISTINGUISHING FEATURES: Rad's body is powered by nuclear fusion; Rad's skin is made up of rock and stone

-POWERS AND ABILITIES-
STRENGTH: Superhuman
SPECIAL SKILLS AND ABILITIES: None
SUPERHUMAN PHYSICAL POWERS: Strength
SUPERHUMAN MENTAL POWERS: None
SPECIAL LIMITATIONS: None
SOURCE OF SUPERHUMAN POWERS: Tenjin Unifailia Ceremony

Shinjū Prelude Rad
Lineart by Travis Stephens

Tag us in your posts!
@kaishostudios

© 2020 Travis Stephens
www.kaishostudios.com

Staci Brigitte

-BIOGRAPHICAL DATA-
REAL NAME: Anastasie (Staci) Brigitte
PLACE OF BIRTH: Venasque, France
AGE: 19
MARITAL STATUS: Single
KNOWN RELATIVES: None known
KNOWN CONFIDANTS: Kosen; Matt Kindle
BASE OF OPERATIONS: Pacific Estate, Crawford, Colorado
CURRENT GROUP MEMBERSHIP: The Tenjin

-PHYSICAL DESCRIPTION-
HEIGHT: 5'0"
WEIGHT: 120 lbs.
EYES: Blue
HAIR: Blonde; Dyed blue & green currently
OTHER DISTINGUISHING FEATURES: None known

-POWERS AND ABILITIES-
STRENGTH: Normal
SPECIAL SKILLS AND ABILITIES: Fluent in French, English, and Russian
SUPERHUMAN PHYSICAL POWERS: None
SUPERHUMAN MENTAL POWERS: Astral Projection
SPECIAL LIMITATIONS: Use of her powers is limited to her mental stamina
SOURCE OF SUPERHUMAN POWERS: Divine gift from Ten'ja

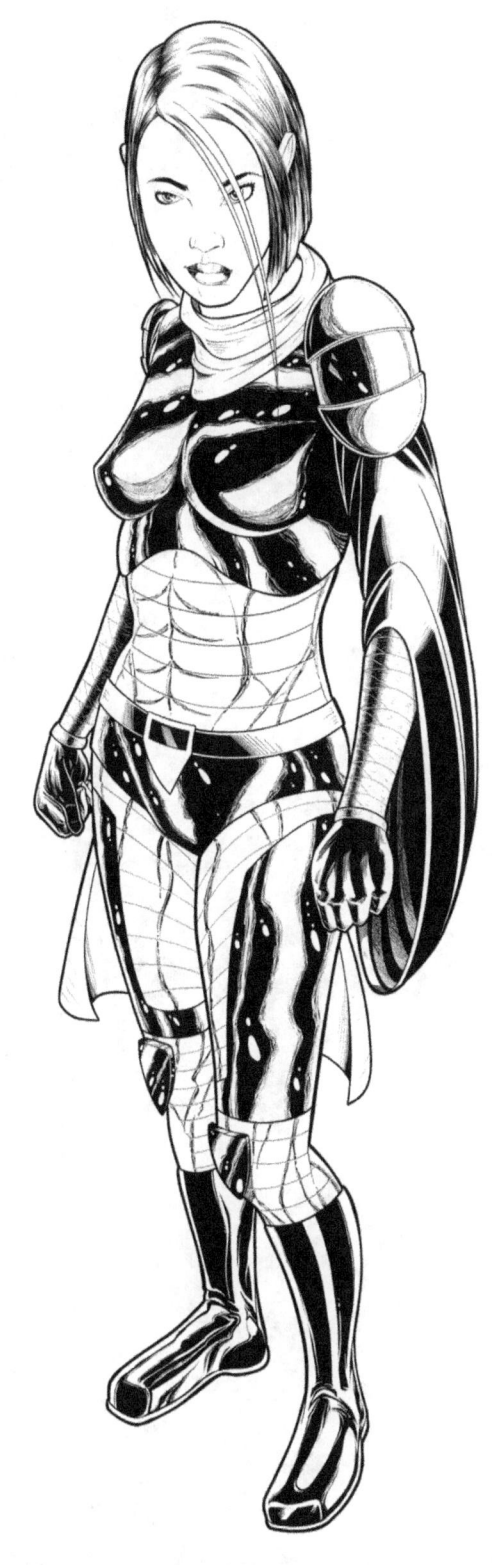

Shinjū Prelude Staci Brigitte
Lineart by Travis Stephens

Tag us in your posts!
@kaishostudios

© 2020 Travis Stephens
www.kaishostudios.com

A

Anders, Ashley-Real name of Tenjin Toa; Sister of Christy Anders.
Anders, Christy-Tenjin warrior with the ability of sorcerey; Sister of Ashley Anders
Astral Projection-The ability to project one's spirit from one's physical body.
Augury-Clairvoyant woman who guides the Pacific Estate Tenjin sect.

B

Banyoro-Caretakers of the Cwezi alters; Temporary vessels for corrupted Tenjin souls.
Brigitte, Anastasia (Staci)-Tenjin warrior with the ability to astral project.

C

Chizan-Title of Tenjin master
Chosen-Superhumans blessed by Ten'ja
Clairvoyance-The ability to perceive things without using the five physical senses.
Cleansing Ceremony-A ritual performed to re-align corrupted Chosen souls.
Copert-Tenjin warrior.
Cwezi-Ancient Gods that reside in the mountains of Uganda.

F

Faceless Ones-Former Chosen that have given up their identity to find peace.
Fire Manipulation-The ability to create fire and expel it from one's body.

H

Healers-Tenjin's gifted with the ability to cure ailments.
Houser-Tenjin warrior.

J

Jūjigun-A war that splintered Cwezi followers into Tenjin and Ujikira sects.

K

Kanneshi-Title of Tenjin sect leader.
Kindle, Matt-Tenjin warrior with the ability to ma
Light Manipulation-The ability to absorb light and expel it in a solid form.

M

Magma Manipulation-The ability to create magma and expel it from your body.
Morphing-The ability to transform into another form.
Mukami-Cwezi god that administers the Tenjin cleansing ritual.

N

Naukara-Ujikira warriors; Banyoro hosts with corrupted souls.
Necromancy-The ability to speak to and raise the dead.
Nikati-Ujikira warrior with the ability of telepathy.

P

Pacific Estate-Tenjin sect located in Crawford, Colorado.

R

Rad-Tenjin warrior with the ability of magma manipulation.
Raider, Joseph-Tenjin warrior with the ability of telepathy and telekinesis.

S

Scourge-Alien invaders that attempted to conquer Earth.
Sorcery-Ancient art of utilizing unknown mystic energies.
Superhuman-A person with abilities and powers beyond human standards.

T

Telekinesis-The ability to move objects without physically touching them.
Telepathy-The ability to send and receive thoughts.
Teleportation-The ability to move objects between two points without traveling that distance.
Teleporters-Tenjin's with the ability to create teleportation portals.
Tenjin-Followers of the Cwezi disciple Ten'ja.
Ten'ja-A disciple of the Cwezi that helped spread their message throughout the world.
Toa-Tenjin warrior with the ability to create light constructs; Code name of Ashley Anders.

U

Ujikira-Followers of the Cwezi disciple Ujin'ce
Ujin'ce-A disciple of the Cwezi that helped spread their message throughout the world.
Unifailia Ceremony-A ritual for Chosen to test one's worthiness of being Tenjin.

Shinjū Prelude Dictionary

Tag us in your posts!
@kaishostudios

© 2020 Travis Stephens
www.kaishostudios.com

www.ingramcontent.com/pod-product-compliance
Lightning Source LLC
Chambersburg PA
CBHW081455220526
45466CB00008B/2658